First World War
and Army of Occupation
War Diary
France, Belgium and Germany

62 DIVISION
Divisional Troops
Royal Army Medical Corps
2/2 West Riding Field Ambulance
9 January 1917 - 31 May 1919

WO95/3078/2

Published by

The Naval & Military Press Ltd

Unit 10 Ridgewood Industrial Park,

Uckfield, East Sussex,

TN22 5QE England

Tel: +44 (0) 1825 749494

www.naval-military-press.com

www.nmarchive.com

This diary has been reprinted in facsimile from the original. Any imperfections are inevitably reproduced and the quality may fall short of modern type and cartographic standards.

© **Crown Copyright**
Images reproduced by permission of The National Archives, London, England, 2015.

Contents

Document type	Place/Title	Date From	Date To
Heading	WO95/3078/2		
Heading	62nd Division 2-2nd (W.R.) Fld Ambulance Jan 1917-1919 May		
Heading	War Diary of 2/2nd West Riding Field Ambulance R.A.M.C. (T) From 9th January 1917 To 31st January 1917 Volume 1		
War Diary	Bedford	09/01/1917	09/01/1917
War Diary	Havre	10/01/1917	11/01/1917
War Diary	Journey (Rail)	12/01/1917	12/01/1917
War Diary	Villers L'Hopital	13/01/1917	22/01/1917
War Diary	Bretel	23/01/1917	23/01/1917
War Diary	Bus-Les Artois	24/01/1917	31/01/1917
Miscellaneous	Appendix No. 1 Medical Services.	14/01/1917	14/01/1917
Miscellaneous	Re Drinking Water		
Miscellaneous	Appendix No 3 Bounds.		
Heading	War Diary of 2/2nd West Riding Field Ambulance From 1st February 1917 To 28th February 1917 (Volume 2)		
War Diary	Bus-Les-Artois	01/02/1917	16/02/1917
War Diary	Acheux	17/02/1917	28/02/1917
Miscellaneous	Appendix No.1 Extract From Regt. Orders 17-3-1917 Accommodation State.	17/02/1917	17/02/1917
Heading	War Diary of 2/2nd West Riding Field Ambce From 1st March 1917 To 31st March 1917 Volume 3		
War Diary	Acheux	01/03/1917	31/03/1917
Heading	War Diary of 2/2nd W.R. Field Ambulance R.A.M.C. (T) From 1.4.17 To 30.4.17 Volume A		
War Diary	Acheux	01/04/1917	03/04/1917
War Diary	Achiet-Le-Grand	04/04/1917	06/04/1917
War Diary	Fork Behagnies	07/04/1917	07/04/1917
War Diary	Behagnies	08/04/1917	08/04/1917
War Diary	Mory	09/04/1917	13/04/1917
War Diary	Ervillers	14/04/1917	30/04/1917
Heading	War Diary of 2/2nd West Riding Field Ambulance From 1st May 1917 To 31st May 1917 Volume 5.		
War Diary	Ervillers	01/05/1917	29/05/1917
War Diary	Behagnies	30/05/1917	31/05/1917
Heading	War Diary of 2/2nd W.R. Field Ambulance R.A.M.C. (T) From 1st June 1917 To 30th June 1917 Volume No 6		
War Diary	Behagnies	01/06/1917	27/06/1917
War Diary	Achiet-Le-Grand	28/06/1917	30/06/1917
Map	Map Reference		
Heading	War Diary of 2/2 W.R. Field Ambce From 1 July To 31 July 1917 Volume 7		
War Diary	Achiet Le Grand	01/07/1917	31/07/1917
Map	Map Reference		
Heading	War Diary of 2/2nd W.R. Field Ambulance R.A.M.C. (T) From 1st Aug 1917 To 31st Aug 1917 Volume 8		
War Diary	Achiet-Le-Grand	01/08/1917	31/08/1917

Heading	War Diary of 2/2nd W.R. Field Ambulance From Sept 1st 1917 To Sept 30th 1917 Volume 9		
War Diary	Achiet-Le-Grand	01/09/1917	30/09/1917
Heading	War Diary of 2/2nd West Riding Field Ambulance R.A.M.C. (T) From 1st Oct 1917 To 31st Oct 1917 Volume 10		
War Diary	Achiet-Le-Grand	01/10/1917	12/10/1917
War Diary	Beaulencourt	13/10/1917	19/10/1917
War Diary	Le Transloy	20/10/1917	31/10/1917
Heading	War Diary of 2/2nd West Riding Field Ambulance From 1st-Nov-1917 To 30th-Nov-1917 Volume No 11		
War Diary	Gouy	01/11/1917	14/11/1917
War Diary	Achiet-Le-Grand	15/11/1917	15/11/1917
War Diary	Bus	16/11/1917	30/11/1917
Heading	2/2 West Riding F.A		
War Diary	Bus	01/12/1917	03/12/1917
War Diary	Bailleulmont	04/12/1917	04/12/1917
War Diary	Montenescourt	05/12/1917	05/12/1917
War Diary	Berles	06/12/1917	09/12/1917
War Diary	Annezin	10/12/1917	14/12/1917
War Diary	Gonnehem	14/12/1917	18/12/1917
War Diary	Annezin	18/12/1917	18/12/1917
War Diary	Bethencourt	19/12/1917	31/12/1917
Heading	2/2nd W.R Field Ambulance War Diary From 1st Jany 1918 To 31st Jany 1918 Volume 13		
War Diary	Bethencourt	01/01/1918	08/01/1918
War Diary	Maroeuil	09/01/1918	31/01/1918
Heading	2/2nd West Riding F.A.		
Heading	War Diary of 2/2 West Riding Field Ambce From Feby 1/1918 To Feby 28/1918 Volume 14		
War Diary	Maroeuil	01/02/1918	10/02/1918
War Diary	Bailleul Aux Cornailles	11/02/1918	28/02/1918
Diagram etc	Maroeuil		
Heading	2/2nd West Riding F.A.		
War Diary	Bailleul Aux Cornailles	01/03/1918	03/03/1918
War Diary	Roclincourt	04/03/1918	23/03/1918
War Diary	Mont. St Eloi	24/03/1918	24/03/1918
War Diary	Warlus	25/03/1918	25/03/1918
War Diary	Bucquoy	26/03/1918	26/03/1918
War Diary	Humbercamps	27/03/1918	30/03/1918
War Diary	St Leger Lauthie	31/03/1918	31/03/1918
Heading	2/2nd West Riding Field Ambulance		
Heading	War Diary of 2/2nd W.R. Field Ambulance From 1st April 1918 To 30th April 1918 Volume 16		
War Diary	St. Leger	01/04/1918	07/04/1918
War Diary	Souastre	08/04/1918	24/04/1918
War Diary	St. Leger	25/05/1918	30/05/1918
Heading	War Diary of 2/2nd W.R. Field Ambulance, From 1st May 1918 To 31st May 1918 Volume 17		
War Diary	St. Leger	02/05/1918	17/05/1918
War Diary	Henu Bienvillers	18/05/1918	18/05/1918
War Diary	Henu	19/05/1918	31/05/1918
Map	Sheet 57d N.E.		
Map	R.A.P Relay Posts		
Miscellaneous	Appendix A		
Diagram etc	2/2 West Riding Field Ambulance		

Miscellaneous	The Cases Collected at "Z" Relay are evacuated	27/05/1918	27/05/1918
Miscellaneous	Supplementary Route		
Heading	War Diary of 2/2nd W.R. Field Ambulance From 1st June To 30th June 1918 Volume 18		
War Diary	Henu	01/06/1918	30/06/1918
Miscellaneous	Distribution of Area Cleared By 2/2nd 11R.		
Heading	War Diary of 2/2nd West Riding Field Ambce From 1st July To 31st July 1918 Volume 19		
War Diary	Henu	01/07/1918	15/07/1918
War Diary	En Route	16/07/1918	17/07/1918
War Diary	Thibie	18/07/1918	18/07/1918
War Diary	Athis	19/07/1918	19/07/1918
War Diary	Champillon	20/07/1918	28/07/1918
War Diary	St Imoges	29/07/1918	31/07/1918
Heading	War Diary of 2/2nd W.R. Field Ambulance From 1st Aug 1918 To 31st Aug 1918 Volume 21		
War Diary	St. Imoges	01/08/1918	01/08/1918
War Diary	Chouilly	02/08/1918	04/08/1918
War Diary	In Train	05/08/1918	05/08/1918
War Diary	Marieux Wood	06/08/1918	14/08/1918
War Diary	Marieux	15/08/1918	19/08/1918
War Diary	Saulty	20/08/1918	21/08/1918
War Diary	Thievres	22/08/1918	23/08/1918
War Diary	Saulty	24/08/1918	24/08/1918
War Diary	Ayette	25/08/1918	31/08/1918
Heading	2/2nd West Riding F.A.		
Heading	War Diary of 2/2nd West Riding Field Ambce From 1st Sept 1918 To 30th Sept 1918 Volume 21		
War Diary	Ayette	01/09/1918	02/09/1918
War Diary	Gommiecourt	03/09/1918	10/09/1918
War Diary	Haplincourt	11/09/1918	16/09/1918
War Diary	Courcelles	17/09/1918	25/09/1918
War Diary	Fremicourt	26/09/1918	27/09/1918
War Diary	Ruyalcourt	28/09/1918	30/09/1918
Diagram etc	Hedge (Limit Of Compound)		
Heading	2/2 West Riding F.A		
War Diary	Ruyalcourt	01/10/1918	03/10/1918
War Diary	Havrincourt	04/10/1918	09/10/1918
War Diary	Masnieres	10/10/1918	10/10/1918
War Diary	Seranvillers	11/10/1918	11/10/1918
War Diary	Carnieres	12/10/1918	17/10/1918
War Diary	Quievy	18/10/1918	31/10/1918
Miscellaneous	Appendix A The Scheme for the evacuation of Wounded up to Zero on the 20 th October 18. was as follows:-	20/10/1918	20/10/1918
Map	Map		
Miscellaneous	Appendix B A brief outline of the scheme of attack was as follows.		
Miscellaneous	Appendix C As the advance Proceeded further the R.A.P s were changed to the following.		
Heading	War Diary of 2/2 West Riding Field Ambce From 1 Oct 1918 To 31 Oct 1918 Volume 22		
Heading	War Diary of 2/2nd West Riding Field Ambulance From 1st Nov 1918 To 30th November 1918 Volume 23		
War Diary	Quievy	01/11/1918	02/11/1918

War Diary	Ruesnes	06/11/1918	07/11/1918
War Diary	Gommegnies	08/11/1918	08/11/1918
War Diary	Obies	09/11/1918	11/11/1918
War Diary	Sous Le Bois	12/11/1918	18/11/1918
War Diary	Colleret	19/11/1918	19/11/1918
War Diary	Biercee	20/11/1918	20/11/1918
War Diary	Somzee	21/11/1918	23/11/1918
War Diary	Nowechamps	24/11/1918	24/11/1918
War Diary	Bioul	25/11/1918	25/11/1918
War Diary	Evrehailles	26/11/1918	26/11/1918
War Diary	Reux	27/11/1918	30/11/1918
Heading	62nd Div Box 2954 2/2nd West Riding F.A.		
War Diary	Reux	01/12/1918	09/12/1918
War Diary	Scy	10/12/1918	10/12/1918
War Diary	Chardeneux	11/12/1918	11/12/1918
War Diary	Ville	12/12/1918	12/12/1918
War Diary	Habimont	13/12/1918	13/12/1918
War Diary	Ennal	14/12/1918	15/12/1918
War Diary	Poteau	16/12/1918	16/12/1918
War Diary	Mirfeld	17/12/1918	21/12/1918
War Diary	Bullingen	22/12/1918	22/12/1918
War Diary	Hellenthal	23/12/1918	23/12/1918
War Diary	Heistert	24/12/1918	24/12/1918
War Diary	Holzheim	25/12/1918	31/12/1918
Heading	2/2nd West Riding F.A.		
War Diary	Holzheim	01/01/1919	31/01/1919
Heading	War Diary of 2/2nd West Riding Field Ambulance From 1st February To 28th February 1919 Volume 27		
War Diary	Holzheim	01/02/1919	28/02/1919
Heading	Mar.1919 2/2nd W. Riding F.A.		
War Diary	Holzheim	01/03/1919	11/03/1919
War Diary	Kelz	12/03/1919	31/03/1919
Heading	War Diary of 2/2nd West Riding Field Ambulance From 1st April, 1919 To 30th April 1919 Volume No. 28.		
War Diary	Kelz	01/04/1919	09/04/1919
War Diary	Duren	10/04/1919	30/04/1919
Heading	War Diary of 2/2nd. West Riding Field Ambulance RAMC (T.F) From 1st May 1919 To 31st May 1919 Volume No. 29		
War Diary	Duren	01/05/1919	23/05/1919
War Diary	Girbelsrath	24/05/1919	31/05/1919

WO95/3078/2

62ND DIVISION

2-2ND (W.R.) FLD AMBULANCE
JAN 1917-DEC 1918
1919 NH3

62ND DIVISION

140/1947

Vol 1

62nd D:

Jan 1917

ORIGINAL

Confidential

War Diary

of

2/2nd West Riding Field Ambulance,
R.A.M.C. (T)

from 9th January 1917 to 31st January 1917

Volume 1.

COMMITTEE FOR THE
MEDICAL HISTORY OF THE WAR
Date 13 MAR. 1917

Army Form C. 2118

(Original)

½ West Riding Field Ambulance

WAR DIARY
or
INTELLIGENCE SUMMARY.
(Erase heading not required.)

Instructions regarding War Diaries and Intelligence Summaries are contained in F. S. Regs., Part II. and the Staff Manual respectively. Title pages will be prepared in manuscript.

Place	Date	Hour	Summary of Events and Information	Remarks and references to Appendices
	1917			
BEDFORD ant CR	9-1-17 Tues.	5 a.m.	Entrained at No. 6 Ballast Pit, BEDFORD for SOUTHAMPTON. Arrived SOUTHAMPTON DOCKS 11:30 a.m. Embarked on the "TEVIOT", an old cargo boat which left the dock at 8 p.m.	
HAVRE ant CR	10-1-17 WED.	12:30 p.m.	Arrived at dock, HAVRE, at 12:30 p.m. Disembarked and marched six miles to REST CAMP No. 2, arriving 9 p.m.	
HAVRE ant CR	11-1-17 THUR.	2:30 p.m.	Left HAVRE station 2:30 p.m. by train. Officers in 2nd Class carriages, men in trucks, 35 per truck. No. 722 Pte. LORD, proceeded to BASE through commencement of No. 2 REST CAMP to D.A. & Q.M.G.'s office as clerk.	
JOURNEY (RAIL) ant CR	12-1-17 FRI.	2:15 a.m.	Halted for 30 minutes to water and feed horses at MONTROLLIER. BUCHY at 2:15 a.m. (4 hours late). Halted again for 30 minutes to water & feed horses at ABBEVILLE at 12 noon (about 5 hours late). Arrived at AUXI-LE-CHATEAU, detrained at 3 p.m. Travelled by road 6 miles to VILLERS L'HOPITAL. Arrived 9 p.m. Went into billets. Officers in peasants' houses. Men in barns.	
VILLERS L'HOPITAL ant CR	13-1-17 SAT.		Remained at VILLERS L'HOPITAL. Opened a Detention Hospital.	

(original)

Army Form C. 2118.

WAR DIARY
or
INTELLIGENCE SUMMARY.
(Erase heading not required.)

1/2 West Riding Field Ambulance

Place	Date	Hour	Summary of Events and Information	Remarks and references to Appendices
VILLERS L'HOPITAL	14.1.17 SUN.		Still at VILLERS L'HOPITAL. Opened up negotiations with No. 16 M.A.C., FREVENT, for removal of patients.	APPENDIX No 1.
VILLERS L'HOPITAL	15.1.17 MON.		Still at VILLERS L'HOPITAL. Seven motor Ambulances, 5 DAIMLER and 2 FORD, reported for duty with this Unit.	APPENDIX No 2.
VILLERS L'HOPITAL	16.1.17 TUES.		Still at VILLERS L'HOPITAL. Orders received that one light motor ambulance must be in attendance at A.D.M.S. office each day from 9 a.m. to 5 p.m. One motor cycle (DOUGLAS) was out of use inside one of the motor ambulances which arrived on the 15th inst. The Revd. Capt. NHITESIDE returned to this Unit after travelling with the 2/5 TH WEST RIDING REGT.	
VILLERS L'HOPITAL	17.1.17 WED.		Paragraphs 1 to 44 of the ARMY ACT were read to the men of this unit on parade. The Revd. Capt. W.T. MOULTON returned to this Unit after travelling overseas with the 2/4TH WEST RIDING REGT. Steel helmets to be worn on all occasions when on duty or marching out.	APPENDIX No 3.

Army Form C. 2118.

(Original)

WAR DIARY
or
INTELLIGENCE SUMMARY.
(Erase heading not required.)

1/6 West Riding Field Ambulance

Instructions regarding War Diaries and Intelligence Summaries are contained in F.S. Regs., Part II. and the Staff Manual respectively. Title pages will be prepared in manuscript.

Place	Date	Hour	Summary of Events and Information	Remarks and references to Appendices
VILLERS L'HOPITAL Off OR	18.1.17 THUR		The whole of the Car helmets of the personnel of unit, attached A.S.C. and M.T. were inspected. Pay was drawn from the Field Cashier (13th Army Corps) Doullens, to the amount of 2,300 francs. Motor Cyclist Despatch Rider, M2/050550 The Heginbotham, F. reported from 62nd D.S.C. Neuvillette, with 2 Motor Bicycle (Douglas) Both were taken on the strength of this Unit accordingly.	
VILLERS L'HOPITAL Off OR	19.1.17 FRI.		Personnel of Unit, A.S.C. and M.T. attached, paid in multiples of five francs.	
VILLERS L'HOPITAL Off OR	20.1.17 SAT.		A composite complete (A) Section of 62 men with four Officers (including the Quarter-Master) proceeded to COIGNEUX for duty and purposes of instruction with the 5½th Field Ambulance 19th Division.	
VILLERS L'HOPITAL Off OR	21.1.17 SUN		Remaining at VILLERS L'HOPITAL	
VILLERS L'HOPITAL Off OR	22.1.17 MON		Marched by road to BRETEL front @ 11" x 5 9' Arrive 11. 1 mile due west of DOULLENS where the unit was billetted in barns for the night.	

WAR DIARY
or
INTELLIGENCE SUMMARY.
(Erase heading not required.)

Army Form C. 2118.

Place	Date	Hour	Summary of Events and Information	Remarks and references to Appendices
BRETEL	23.1.17 Tues		Continued march by road from BRETEL to BUS-LES-ARTOIS. Found © 33' x D "7" where the Unit took up quarters at the hospital	
BUS-LES-ARTOIS	24.1.17 Wed.		Unit at BUS-LES-ARTOIS. Opened the hospital as Retention hospital for the sick of the area. Casualties being treated elsewhere.	
BUS-LES-ARTOIS	25.1.17 Thurs		The C.O. proceeded to AMIENS to arrange about laundry work being done there. An officer of this Unit Lt VAUGHAN was appointed by the ADMS to supervise the Unit's working order. The baths at LOUVENCOURT, ROSSIGNOL FARM BUS and AUTHIE. The A and A. 5th Army wanted the hospital in arrangements at the request of the Y.M.C.A. for this Unit to supply them with the required amount of tea & water.	
BUS-LES-ARTOIS	26.1.17 Fri.		Unit at BUS-LES-ARTOIS.	
BUS-LES-ARTOIS	27.1.17 Sat.		Four men detailed to do duty in the Y.M.C.A. huts.	
BUS-LES-ARTOIS	28.1.17 Sun.			
BUS-LES-ARTOIS	29.1.17 Mon		The complete "A" Section returned to this UNIT from COIGNEUX where it was temporarily attached to the 57th Field Ambulance for evacuational	

Army Form C. 2118.

WAR DIARY
or
INTELLIGENCE SUMMARY.
(Erase heading not required.)

(original) 1/2 West Riding Field Ambulance

Place	Date	Hour	Summary of Events and Information	Remarks and references to Appendices
BUS-LES-ARTOIS W.R.O.	29.1.17 Mon.		Purposes being replaced by a further complete section composed of 3 Officers and 60 men. An officer of this unit Lieut. SINNETTE was detailed by the D.D.M.S. to act as Sanitary Advisor to the Town Major.	
BUS-LES-ARTOIS W.R.O.	30.1.17 Tues.		The Bacterial 5th Army pond arrant to this hospital. The feed bacteria rated BUS-LES-ARTOIS, when ay was drawn to the amount of 2550 francs.	
BUS-LES-ARTOIS W.R.O.	31.1.17 Wed.		2nd.C.O. Unit proceeded to COIGNEUX to visit the 57th field Amb to inspect minn road the brewing stations.	

APPENDIX No. 1.

MEDICAL SERVICES.

SICK.
Each Field Ambulance will open a small Detention Hospital for the treatment of cases which do not require detention beyond THREE DAYS. Accommodation will be provided for scabies patients. The latter will be treated by means of scabies cabinets which must be provided immediately, one for each Ambulance Material should be obtained from the C.R.E.
Bad cases of scabies will be sent to No. 6 Stationary Hospital, FREVENT.
Infectious cases, including C.S.M., to No. 12 Stationary Hospital, St. POL.
A Motor Cyclist will call daily at the Ambulances to ask what motor ambulance accommodation is required.
Infectious cases will not be sent to the Detention Hospitals previous to removal to Hospiyal. They will be immediately reported to O.C. nearest Field Ambulance who will arrange for their removal.
Motor Ambulances required for very urgent cases can be obtained from No. 16 Motor Ambulance Convoy, FREVENT.

Sick should be sent to the nearest Field Ambulance.
C.S.M. cases should be immediately reported to the A.D.M.S. by wire.

Replenishment of Medical Stores.
A.F.I. 1209 (in duplicate) should be sent to No. 13 Advanced Depot Medical Stores, DOULLENS, transport being sent at same time.
Medical Officers i/c Units will indent on O.C. nearest Field Ambulance.

16-1-17

AUTHOR:— T.C. LUCAS, MAJOR, RAMC
for COL., A.D.M.S, 62ND DIVISION.

APPENDIX 2.

Re DRINKING WATER.

No water, from whatever source, (wells, streams etc.) must be used for drinking purposes without having been previously chlorinated or boiled. The following notice has been put up on all wells in the district:-
"This water must not be used by troops for drinking purposes."

The above order applies equally to milk. No milk is to be purchased in the village.

EAMES,
(sd) C.W. , Lt.Col. RAMCT.
Commg. 2/2nd. West Riding
Field Ambulance.

APPENDIX No. 3.

BOUNDS.

No N.C.O. or man, except on duty, will leave the Billeting Area of his Unit without a pass. N.C.O's and men on pass will carry a rifle and wear a Bandolier. N.C.O's & men will be in billets by 7 p.m. No N.C.O. or man will proceed for any purpose a distance of 300 yards from his billets without his rifle and ammunition.

STEEL HELMETS.

Men have been noticed wearing their steel helmet lining as a cap, which practice must cease forthwith. It is forbidden to remove the lining from the steel helmet. Steel helmets will be worn at all times by all ranks engaged in operations. When troops are not engaged in operations steel helmets will be worn by all ranks on guard, on parade, when training or on the march.

EXTRACTS FROM
62ND. Divl. Standing Orders.

ORIGINAL

62nd Div.

Confidential

War Diary

— OF —

2/2ND West Riding Field Ambulance.

FROM. 1st February 1914. TO. 26th February 1914.

(Volume K.)

Vol 2

COMMITTEE FOR THE
MEDICAL HISTORY OF THE WAR
Date 4 — APR. 1917

Army Form C. 2118.

WAR DIARY
or
INTELLIGENCE SUMMARY.
(Erase heading not required.)

2/2nd West Riding Field Ambulance

Original

Place	Date	Hour	Summary of Events and Information	Remarks and references to Appendices
BUS-LES-ARTOIS	1-2-17 Thurs.	a.m.	Still remaining at BUS-LES-ARTOIS.	
BUS-LES-ARTOIS	2-2-17 Friday	a.m.	Still remaining at BUS-LES-ARTOIS.	
BUS-LES-ARTOIS	3-2-17 Sat.	a.m.	The composite section attached to the 57th Field Ambulance for instructional purposes at the Advanced Dressing Station returned to this Unit and were replaced by the 5th and last composite section.	
		a.m.	Lieut. M.B.G. SINNETTE proceeded to BERTRANCOURT for temporary duty with the H.A.G.	
BUS-LES-ARTOIS	4-2-17 SUN.	a.m.	a/ officers and 15 men of this Unit proceeded to VAUCHELLE for temporary duty with the 91st Field Ambulance.	
BUS-LES-ARTOIS	5-2-17 MON.	a.m.	Still remaining at BUS-LES-ARTOIS.	
BUS-LES-ARTOIS	6-2-17 TUES.	a.m.	Capt. W.J.L. HICKEY reported to the 2/4 West Riding Regt. for duty as M.O.	
BUS-LES-ARTOIS	7-2-17 WED.	a.m.	Two men (R.A.M.C.) reported to this Unit from the BASE as reinforcements to establishment.	
BUS-LES-ARTOIS	8-2-17 THURS.	a.m.	Still remaining at BUS-LES-ARTOIS.	

Army Form C. 2118.

2/2nd West Riding Field Ambulance

WAR DIARY
or
INTELLIGENCE SUMMARY.
(Erase heading not required.)

ORIGINAL

Instructions regarding War Diaries and Intelligence Summaries are contained in F. S. Regs., Part II. and the Staff Manual respectively. Title pages will be prepared in manuscript.

Place	Date	Hour	Summary of Events and Information	Remarks and references to Appendices
BUS-LES-ARTOIS	9-2-17 FRIDAY	a.m.	The Composite Section attached to the 57th Field Ambulance at COIGNEUX returned to this Unit after six days instructional work in the trenches and advanced Dressing Station. CAPT. A.M. DAVIE proceeded on temporary duty as M.O. i/c. 2/5th West Yorkshire Regt.	
BUS-LES-ARTOIS	10-2-17 SAT.	a.m.	Still remaining at BUS-LES-ARTOIS.	
BUS-LES-ARTOIS	11-2-17 SUN	a.m.	Still remaining at BUS-LES-ARTOIS. Three drivers, A.S.C.M.T., reported for duty with this unit from the 62nd Divn. Supply Column Workshops. A Sergeant of this unit was detailed for duty at the Brigade Baths as an inspector for scabies.	
BUS-LES-ARTOIS	12-2-17 MON	a.m.	A further detachment of eight N.C.O's + men of this Unit reported to the 91st Field Ambulance for duty.	
BUS-LES-ARTOIS	13-2-17 TUES.	a.m.	Still remaining at BUS-LES-ARTOIS.	
BUS-LES-ARTOIS	14-2-17 WED	a.m.	One officer and eighteen N.C.O's men proceeded to ACHEUX as advance party to take over the hospital	

Army Form C. 2118.

WAR DIARY
or
INTELLIGENCE SUMMARY.
(Erase heading not required.)

2/2nd West Riding Field Ambulance — ORIGINAL

Place	Date	Hour	Summary of Events and Information	Remarks and references to Appendices
Bus-les-ARTOIS	14-2-17 WED		Here as a Corps Rest Station from the 92nd Field Ambulance	
Bus-les-ARTOIS	15-2-17 THURS	Cont.	Still remaining at Bus-les-Artois	
Bus-les-ARTOIS	16-2-17 FRI	Cont.	This Unit handed over the hospital at Bus-les-Artois to the 2/3rd West Riding Field Ambulance and proceeded to ACHEUX to carry on the work at the Corps Rest Station there, taken over from the 92nd Field Ambulance. Three officers and thirty-two NCO's & men of the 58th Field Ambulance who had been attached to the 92nd Field Ambulance for duty at the Corps Rest Station went spersely attached to do so for the same duty upon taking over. Three Sub officers (one each from the 58th, 92nd and 2/3rd (W.R.) Field Ambulances respectively) were attached to the Company Rooms Staff for purposes of keeping the R.A.M.C. books for their respective divisions. Two nursing orderlies were sent to GEZAINCOURT to report to the Officers' Hospital there for temporary duty	

Army Form C. 2118.

WAR DIARY
or
INTELLIGENCE SUMMARY.
(Erase heading not required.)

Instructions regarding War Diaries and Intelligence Summaries are contained in F.S. Regs., Part II. and the Staff Manual respectively. Title pages will be prepared in manuscript.

2/2nd West Riding Field Ambulance

ORIGINAL

Place	Date	Hour	Summary of Events and Information	Remarks and references to Appendices
ACHEUX	17-2-17 SAT	CWE	Remaining at ACHEUX. One Ford and one Daimler Ambulance with two drivers and two orderlies of this unit were sent to BERTRANCOURT to report for duty with the 2/1st W.R. Field Ambulance stationed there. This unit arranged to supply 100 gallons of water daily to the Y.M.C.A.	APPENDIX I.
ACHEUX	18-2-17 SUN	CWE	Still remaining at ACHEUX. One man of this unit reported to the 31st Kite Balloon Section, R.F.C., near COUIN, for duty with that unit.	
ACHEUX	19-2-17 MON	CWE	Still remaining at ACHEUX. Capt. N.T. WHITEHEAD, R.A.M.C. reported for temporary duty from the 1st Stationary Hospital. A further Daimler Ambulance together with one driver and one wagon orderly was sent to BERTRANCOURT to report for duty to the 2/1st W.R. Field Ambulance there	
ACHEUX	20-2-17 TUES	CWE	Still remaining at ACHEUX	
ACHEUX	21-2-17 WED	CWE	Still remaining at ACHEUX. Capt. A.M. DAVIE, R.A.M.C.T. returned to the unit from temporary duty as M.O. yc 2/5th West Yorks Regt.	

Army Form C. 2118.

WAR DIARY
or
INTELLIGENCE SUMMARY.
(Erase heading not required.)

2/3rd West Riding Field Ambulance

ORIGINAL

Instructions regarding War Diaries and Intelligence Summaries are contained in F.S. Regs, Part II. and the Staff Manual respectively. Title pages will be prepared in manuscript.

Place	Date	Hour	Summary of Events and Information	Remarks and references to Appendices
ACHEUX	22-2-17 THURS.	C.W.R	Still remaining at ACHEUX.	
ACHEUX	23-2-17 FRI.	C.W.R	Still remaining at ACHEUX. This Unit now in addition to the working of a Corps Rest Station to take charge of the sick of the 62nd Division, forming a Divisional Field Hospital.	
ACHEUX	24-2-17 SAT.	C.W.R	Still remaining at ACHEUX.	
ACHEUX	25-2-17 SUN.	C.W.R	Still remaining at ACHEUX. The N.C.O.s were doing duty with the 91st Field Ambulance returned to this Unit. Capt. B. HOLROYD, R.A.M.C.(T) and a Bearer Sub-section left this Unit and proceeded to MAILLY to do duty with the 2/1st (W.R.) Field Ambulance.	
ACHEUX	26-2-17 MON.	C.W.R	Still remaining at ACHEUX. Capt. H.F. STRICKLAND, R.A.M.C. reported for duty from the 58th Field Ambulance to relieve Capt. JOHNSON, R.A.M.C. of the same Unit, who was ordered to return to this Unit for former duties.	
ACHEUX	27-2-17 TUES.	C.W.R	Still remaining at ACHEUX.	

Army Form C. 2118.

WAR DIARY
or
INTELLIGENCE SUMMARY.
(Erase heading not required.)

2nd West Riding Field Ambulance

ORIGINAL

Place	Date	Hour	Summary of Events and Information	Remarks and references to Appendices
ACHEUX	28.2.17 WED	7 aℳ	Still remaining at ACHEUX. The Corps Rest Station now to be changed to a Collecting Station for the entraining of walking wounded for the 5th Army. Capt A.G. HEBBLETHWAITE, R.A.M.C. being appointed Entraining Medical Officer.	

E. W. Ames —
Lieut. Colonel, R.A.M.C. (T)
Commanding 2/2nd W.R. Field Ambulance.

2/2nd West Riding Field Ambulance,
R.A.M.C. (T)

APPENDIX N°. 1.
EXTRACT FROM REGTL. ORDERS 17-2-1917.

ACCOMMODATION STATE

Wardmasters are responsible for notifying Receiving Room of the number of vacant beds in their respective Wards at 8.0am, 12 noon and 4 pm daily.

TRANSFERS to C.C.S.

All transfers to C.C. Station are marked by the M.O. on his morning round, walking cases are paraded at the Receiving tent at 2.15 pm daily by their respective Wardmasters for approval of the O.C. The location of Lying cases are also given at this parade so that the O.C. can see them. Where transfers to C.C.S. have been approved by the O.C. Wardmasters collect the Field Medical Cards and send them to the office so that the evacuation wire may be prepared for D.D.M.S. Field Medical Cards of C.C.S cases must have the ward number on back of card and state on front of them whether the patients are going as lying or sitting cases. M.A.C. Cars arrive for these evacuations between 10.30 & 11.30 am. The D.D.M.S. orders these cars in accordance with the wire sent from C.R.S. the previous evening.

AUTHOR - LIEUT. COL. C.W. EAMES, R.A.M.C.T.
O.C. V CORPS REST STATION.

Original.

C in old Pen.

Mar. 1917

140/1042

No 3

CONFIDENTIAL

COMMITTEE FOR THE
MEDICAL HISTORY OF THE WAR
Date 11 MAY.1917

War Diary.

of

2/2nd West Riding Field Amb^{ce}.

From 1st March 1917. to 31st March 1917.

Volume 3

WAR DIARY
INTELLIGENCE SUMMARY

Army Form C. 2118.

2/2nd W.R. Field Ambulance.
R.A.M.C. (T)

Original   VOLUME 3   SHEET 1.

Place	Date	Hour	Summary of Events and Information	Remarks and references to Appendices
ACHEUX	1/3/17 (THURS)		The Officers & Men of the 58th Field Ambulance attached to this Unit returned to their own Unit for duty. One of our NCOs proceeded to ENGLAND to form the 1st Officers Cader Battalion at BATH. Six mules with their Drivers were attached to the 2/1st WEST RIDING FIELD AMBULANCE being provided with poor Jaudlin. The FORD and DAIMLER Ambulance Cars temporarily attached with Drivers and Negon Orderlies to the 2/1st WEST RIDING FIELD AMBULANCE were returned to this Unit.	
ACHEUX	2/3/17 (FRI.)		Nothing to record.	
ACHEUX	3/3/17 (SAT.)		Captain T.R. KENWORTHY. RAMC(T). proceeded to join the 2/4th YORKS & LANCS. Regiment for temporary duty as MEDICAL OFFICER vice MAJOR BARBER RAMC(T) who had become incapacitated for duty.	

Army Form C. 2118.

2/2nd W.R. Field Ambulance.
R.A.M.C. (T)

WAR DIARY
INTELLIGENCE SUMMARY.
(Erase heading not required.)

Original.

SHEET 2.

Instructions regarding War Diaries and Intelligence Summaries are contained in F.S. Regs., Part II. and the Staff Manual respectively. Title pages will be prepared in manuscript.

Place	Date	Hour	Summary of Events and Information	Remarks and references to Appendices
ACHEUX	4/3/17 (Sun.)	a.m.	CAPTAIN WHITEHEAD R.A.M.C. temporarily attached for duty to this Unit reported for duty as Medical Officer of the 42nd H.A.G.	
ACHEUX	5/3/17 (Mon.)	a.m.	An N.C.O. of this Unit reported to the 187 Infantry Brigade H.Q. for duty as Sanitary Corporal. Nothing to record.	
ACHEUX	6/3/17 (Tues)	a.m.	Nothing to record.	
ACHEUX	7/3/17 (Wed)	a.m.	CAPTAIN HOLROYD B. R.A.M.C. returned to this Unit from temporary duty with the 2/1 WEST RIDING FIELD AMBULANCE.	
ACHEUX	8/3/17 (Thurs)	a.m.	Three men of this Unit were attached for temporary duty as extra stretcher bearers to the Artillery (one per Brigade)	
ACHEUX	9/3/17 (Fri.)	a.m.	Nothing to record.	
ACHEUX	10/3/17 (Sat.)	a.m.	One of the men of the Unit reported with Motor Transport driver, & 2 mules, for duty to the Camp Commandant, 62nd Div. H.Q. ENGLEBELMER. A N.C.O. of this Unit attended a special course of Gas Instruction at 62nd Div. Gas School.	
ACHEUX	11/3/17 (Sun.)	a.m.	Nothing to record.	

WAR DIARY
or
INTELLIGENCE SUMMARY.

Army Form C. 2118.

212nd W.R. Field Ambulance.
R.A.M.C. (T)

Original

SHEET 3.

Place	Date	Hour	Summary of Events and Information	Remarks and references to Appendices
ACHEUX	12/3/17 (MON.)	Cont	A Rest Hospital having been opened at VAUCHELLES the Unit ceased to carry on the duty of I Corps Rest station, the Hospital at ACHEUX now being 62nd Divisional Field Hospital, and a Collecting Station for "Walking Wounded" only.	
ACHEUX	13/3/17 (TUES)	Cont	Nothing to record.	
ACHEUX	14/3/17 (WED.)	Cont	A further Bearer Sub-Division (36 NCOs & Men) reported to the 2/15th WEST RIDING FIELD AMBULANCE from this Unit for duty in the trenches.	
ACHEUX	15/3/17 (THURS)	Cont	CAPTAIN HOLROYD.B RAMC(T) of this Unit reported to the 62nd Divisional Ammunition Column as temporary Medical Officer vice LIEUTENANT WILLIAMS RAMC(T) incapacitated for duty.	
ACHEUX	16/3/17 (FRI)	Cont	Nothing to record.	
ACHEUX	17/3/17 (SAT)	Cont	— do —	
ACHEUX	18/3/17 (SUN)	Cont	— do —	
ACHEUX	19/3/17 (MON.)	Cont	— do —	

Army Form C. 2118.

WAR DIARY
or
INTELLIGENCE SUMMARY.

(Erase heading not required.)

Original.

2/2nd W.R. Field Ambulance.
R.A.M.C. (1)

SHEET 4.

Place	Date	Hour	Summary of Events and Information	Remarks and references to Appendices
ACHEUX	20/3/17 (TUES)	am	Two men reported to this Unit from the 208 Machine Gun Coy. for training in Water duties.	
ACHEUX			LIEUTENANT SINNETTE M.B.G. R.A.M.C. of this Unit is now permanently attached as Medical Officer in charge of the 32nd H.A.G.	
ACHEUX	21/3/17 (WED)	am	Two Lewis Gun carriages are added to the equipment of this Unit.	
			One N.C.O. and 2 men reported at the LANCASHIRE DUMP AVELUY WOOD as a Holding Party for this Unit.	
ACHEUX	22/3/17 (THURS)	am	The Motor Ambulances on duty with the 71 WEST RIDING FIELD AMBULANCE together with drivers & wagon orderlies were returned for duty to this Unit	
ACHEUX	23/3/17 (FRID)	7.0am	Nothing to report.	
ACHEUX	24/3/17 (SAT)	am	CAPT. J. ANDERSON. A. R.A.M.C(T). 4 N.C.O.s + 6 men proceeded to ENGLEBELMER to open 62nd Divisional Rest Station. Also 1 Motor Ambulance.	
			612 Pte. PARKINSON. E. is transferred to 5 Field Training Coy + struck off the strength of this Unit from 21.3.17	

Army Form C. 2118.

2/2nd W.R. Field Ambulance.
R.A.M.C. (T)

WAR DIARY
or
INTELLIGENCE SUMMARY.
(Erase heading not required.)

Original   SHEET 5.

Instructions regarding War Diaries and Intelligence Summaries are contained in F. S. Regs., Part II. and the Staff Manual respectively. Title pages will be prepared in manuscript.

Place	Date	Hour	Summary of Events and Information	Remarks and references to Appendices
ACHEUX	25/3/17 (Sun)		To conform with French Government "Summer time" introduced our clocks & watches advanced 60 Mins. At 11 pm 1 NCO & 11 men returned to this Unit from duty with the 3/1 WEST RIDING FIELD AMBULANCE. On the Wheelhouse evacuated from 11 WR & 9 Sn per Amb. Train. 22 to Base 2 N.T. & taken off the Strength of this Unit that day. 6 men (no reinforcements) reported from base. CAPT. SHARRARD R.A.M.C(T) 2/3 WEST RIDING FIELD AMBULANCE reported to this Unit for duty	
ACHEUX	26/3/17 (Mon)		1 G.S. wagon, 2 HD Horses, 1 Rider & 2 Nurses O.S. Cataract ENGLISHE DRIVER reported to 1/2nd Divisional Nat. Division for temporary duty with this Unit	
ACHEUX	27/3/17 (Tues)		Nothing to record.	

Army Form C. 2118.

WAR DIARY
or
INTELLIGENCE SUMMARY.
(Erase heading not required.)

Original

2/2nd W.R. Field Ambulance
R.A.M.C. (T)

SHEET 6.

Place	Date	Hour	Summary of Events and Information	Remarks and references to Appendices
ACHEUX	Oct 27/17 (WED)		18 men reported back to this Unit from 2/1 West Riding Field Ambulance having been on temporary duty	
ACHEUX	Oct 28/17 (THURS)		27 Other ranks reported back from temporary duty with the 2/1 West Rid. Field Ambulance.	
ACHEUX	Oct 30/17		Nothing to record.	
ACHEUX	Oct 31/17		One (1) A.S.C. (M.T.) attached reported back to his Unit from temporary duty with 62nd Div: A.D.M.S. 6 mules & 6 drivers (A.S.C. H.T. attached) reported back to Unit from duty with the 2/1 West Riding Field Ambulance	

G W Ramer
Lieut. Colonel, R.A.M.C.(T)
Commanding 2/2nd W.R. Field Ambulance.

ORIGINAL

April 1917
62nd Div:

140/2086 / Vol 4

Confidential

War Diary

Of

2/2nd W.R. Field Ambulance,
R.A.M.C. (T)

COMMITTEE FOR THE
MEDICAL HISTORY OF THE WAR
Date = 6 JUN. 1917

From 1·4·17 to 30·4·17

Volume A.

ORIGINAL

Army Form C. 2118.

WAR DIARY
or
INTELLIGENCE SUMMARY.
(Erase heading not required.)

Instructions regarding War Diaries and Intelligence Summaries are contained in F. S. Regs., Part II. and the Staff Manual respectively. Title pages will be prepared in manuscript.

Lieut. Colonel, R.A.M.C.(T)
Commanding 2/2nd W.R. Field Ambulance

VOLUME 4   SHEET 1

Place	Date	Hour	Summary of Events and Information	Remarks and references to Appendices
ACHEUX	1/4/17 (SUN)	a.m.	One N.C.O. and 7 men proceeded to ACHIET-LE-GRAND as baggage party. One N.C.O. was attached to 62nd Division Head Quarters for rations. One other rank A.S.C. attached joined A.S.C. Base Depot HAVRE and was struck off strength of Unit.	
ACHEUX	2/4/17 (MON)	a.m.	Lieut. WILLIAMS. L.A. was discharged from LOUVENCOURT Officers Rest Hospital. One Heavy Draft horse died and was taken off strength. 2 N.C.O's and 17 men proceeded to ACHIET-LE-GRAND	
ACHEUX	3/4/17 (TUES)	a.m.	Capt. SHARRARD returned to the 2/3 West Riding Field Ambulance	
ACHIET-LE-GRAND	4/4/17 (WED)	a.m.	Opened a New Dressing Station at the Brickfields ACHIET-LE-GRAND at noon and took over the Advanced Dressing Station at ERVILLERS (Capt. ANDERSON in charge with one bearer section) Also the Advanced Dressing Station at ST. LEGER (CAPT. POPE from the 2/1 West Riding Field Ambulance attached in charge.) Also Advanced Dressing Station at MORY (CAPT. DAVIE in charge). All the above Advanced Dressing Stations were taken over from the 23rd Field Ambulance, 7th Division.	

Army Form C. 2118.

WAR DIARY
or
INTELLIGENCE SUMMARY.
(Erase heading not required.)

Lieut. Colonel, R.A.M.C.(T)
Commanding 2/2nd W.R. Field Ambulance

SHEET 2

Instructions regarding War Diaries and Intelligence Summaries are contained in F.S. Regs., Part II. and the Staff Manual respectively. Title pages will be prepared in manuscript.

Place	Date	Hour	Summary of Events and Information	Remarks and references to Appendices
ACHIET-LE-GRAND.	4/4/17 (WED.)	On R	2 Bearer subdivisions from the 2/1 and 2/3 West Riding Field Ambulances attached to this Unit for duty.	
	5/4/17 (THUR)	On R	A tenting party was sent to the 2/1 West Riding Field Ambulance post at LOGEAST WOOD. The N.C.O's and men detached with the 2/1 West Riding Field Ambulance working at the A.D.S "20 Ft DROP" were relieved by Capt. BLACKBURN. R.A.M.C.(T) Officer in charge.	
ACHIET-LE-GRAND		On R	M.E. KILLERBY being previously mentioned for devotion to duty while in the line. 2 N.C.O's and 5 men of 526 C. Divisional Train attached, reported to this Unit for duty.	
ACHIET-LE-GRAND	6/4/17 (FRI)	On R	Main Dressing Station moved from Brickfields ACHIET-LE-GRAND to FORK BEHAGNIES SAPIGNIES Road and opened at 6 p.m. The local unit at the last I.M.O Station, sent to Divisional Rest Station and Casualty Clearing Station respectively.	
FORK BEHAGNIES.	7/4/17 (SAT)	On R	Capt. KENNWORTHY T.R. reported back to this Unit for duty from the 2/4 York Lancs, Walking Wounded Dressing Station established at the Fork on the SAPIGNIES, MORY and SAPIGNIES - ERVILLERS Roads, for walking wounded from MORY and ST. LEGER with 6 N.C.O's and men, in charge of Capt. DAVIE and Capt. KENNWORTHY.	
BEHAGNIES	8/4/17 (SUN)	On R	Capt. SICHEL A.N and Capt. TRAILL A. posted to this Unit for duty Ordered to move M.D.S from FORK BEHAGNIES - SAPIGNIES Rd. to ERVILLERS.	

Army Form C. 2118.

WAR DIARY
or
INTELLIGENCE SUMMARY.
(Erase heading not required.)

Lieut. Colonel, R.A.M.C.
Commanding 2/2nd W.R. Field Ambulance.

SHEET 3

Place	Date	Hour	Summary of Events and Information	Remarks and references to Appendices
MORY.	9/4/17 (MON)		Opened M.D.S. at MORY at 6p.m. and established A.D.S. at ECOUST (Capt TRAIL in charge). Also Bearer relays 500 yards long on SUCERIE - ECOUST Road from MORY. Also 2 horse ambulances to meet cases at SUCERIE for MORY, and half a Bearer subdivision left at ERVILLERS with 2 horse ambulances. Also A.D.S. STEEGER with 2 horse ambulances (3 horse ambulances 2/1 West Riding F.Amb. and 12 H.D. horses attached). The Field Ambulance Cars at ERVILLERS as MORY - ERVILLERS Rd. too bad. 2 Ford Cars sent to MORY. Our complete Bearer sub division (with Capt. KENNWORTHY in charge), with 6 pack mules (loaded with stretchers and dressings) ready to move instantly and at disposal of G.O.C. 185 Brigade H.Q. at "L. HOMME MORT."	
MORY.	10/4/17 (TUES)		Cpl. 37/96 Pte STEWART. N. Temporary attached for duty from the 22nd Field Ambulance. 2 H.D. Horses and 1 mule Struck off Strength	
MORY.	11/4/17 (WED)		Lt. Col. BROWN. R.A.M.C. Officer Commanding 2/1 Field Ambulance. reported at M.D.S. MORYABBEY. with 3 officers and 3 Bearer subdivisions assuming Command of the M.D. Station.	
MORY.	12/4/17 (THUR)		Nothing to record.	

Army Form C. 2118.

WAR DIARY
or
INTELLIGENCE SUMMARY.
(Erase heading not required.)

Lieut. Colonel, R.A.M.C.
Commanding 2/2nd W. R. Field Ambulance

SHEET 14

Instructions regarding War Diaries and Intelligence Summaries are contained in F. S. Regs., Part II. and the Staff Manual respectively. Title pages will be prepared in manuscript.

Place	Date	Hour	Summary of Events and Information	Remarks and references to Appendices
MORY	13/4/17 (FRID)	am	1865 Pte LITTLEWOOD. J. admitted to 2/2 West Riding Field Ambulance Hospital suffering from shrapnel wound of shoulder (slight). Head Quarters of Unit moved from MORY ABBEY to ERVILLERS. Col. EAMES. R.A.M.C.(T) taking command of Walking Wounded Station.	
ERVILLERS	14/4/17 (SAT)	am	The M.D.S. at MORY lowered 63rd Division and 7th Division with Col. BROWN 23 Field Ambulance in charge. This under the A.D.M.S. 7th Division. The Walking Wounded Station at ERVILLERS with Col. EAMES 2/2 West Riding F. Ambulance in charge under A.D.M.S. 62nd Division. Officers, NCO's & men from the 2/2 West Riding Field Ambulance and 23rd Field Amb. working M.D.S. MORY and Walking Wounded Dressing Stn ERVILLERS conjointly. The general idea being 62nd Division in exchange of Left Sector & 7th Division in charge of Right Sector.	
ERVILLERS	15/4/17 (SUN)	am	Capt. McKENZIE. R.A.M.C.(T) of the 2/1 West Riding Field Ambulance reported for temporary duty. Lt. VALLON. R.A.M.C.(T) of this Unit reported back from temporary duty with Z. Mobile Laboratory MILLINCOURT. Capt. HOLROYD. R.A.M.C.(T) reported from Officers Hospital WARLOY. One other rank reported for duty from the 2/1 West Riding Field Ambulance.	

Army Form C. 2118.

WAR DIARY
or
INTELLIGENCE SUMMARY.
(Erase heading not required.)

Lieut. Colonel, R.A.M.C.
Commanding 2/2nd W.R. Field Ambulance

SHEET 5

Place	Date	Hour	Summary of Events and Information	Remarks and references to Appendices
ERVILLERS	16/4/17 (MON)	ant	One other rank R.A.M.C, 1 other rank A.S.C. attached with Water Cart and 1 Mule reported back from duty with Camp Commandant 62nd Division.	
ERVILLERS	17/4/17 (TUES)	ant	One mule evacuated by Camp Commandant sick and is struck off strength.	
ERVILLERS	18/4/17 (WED)	ant	324 A/Sgt Major McCANDLISH. J.W. admitted to 2/3 West Riding Field Ambulance Hosp (Sick). One other rank attached from 2/1 West Rid. Ambulance reports back to his Unit.	
ERVILLERS	19/4/17 (THUR)	ant	2 Motor Ambulances attached from 2/3 W.R.F.A returned to their Unit. 2 Other ranks transferred to 312 Brigade R.F.A for water duties. One N.C.O proceeded on 1 months leave on re-engagement.	
ERVILLERS	20/4/17 (FRID)	ant	Nothing to record.	
	21/4/17 (SAT)	ant	Nothing to record.	
	22/4/17 (SUN)	ant	Nothing to record.	
ERVILLERS	23/4/17 (MON)	ant	324 A/Sgt Major McCANDLISH J.W. evacuated to C.C. Station VARENNES 19/4/17 (Sick). 1850 Pte McWILLIAM of this Unit admitted to hospital, shrapnel wound, hand (left) 23/4/17 and discharged same day.	
ERVILLERS	24/4/17 (TUES)	ant	CAPT. HOLROYD. reported for temporary duty to 2/4 Kings Own Light Infantry 24/4/17.	

Army Form C. 2118.

WAR DIARY
or
INTELLIGENCE SUMMARY.
(Erase heading not required.)

Lieut. Colonel, R.A.M.C.
Commanding 2/2nd W.R. Field Ambulance

SHEET 6

Place	Date	Hour	Summary of Events and Information	Remarks and references to Appendices
ERVILLERS	24/4/17 (TUES)	Col	One Ford and 1 Daimler Ambulance Car reported for duty from 2/1 West R. Field Amb. One Daimler reported for duty from the 2/3 West Riding Field Ambulance. Up to this date only few wounded have passed through this Walking Wounded Station.	
ERVILLERS	25/4/17 (WED)	Col	Nothing to record	
	26/4/17		7 Other Ranks reported from Base as reinforcements.	
ERVILLERS (THUR)	27/4/17	Col	Nothing to record	
ERVILLERS	28/4/17	Col	Lt Vallow. RAMC(T) reported to D.M.S. 3rd Army before assuming command of No 16 Mobile (Bac.) Laboratory. Re evacuation of Walking Wounded altered from C.C.S. COLINCAMPS to C.C.S. ACHIET-LE-GRAND.	
ERVILLERS	29/4/17	Col	Nothing to record	
ERVILLERS	30/4/17	Dr 2	Numbers of wounded passing through still very small.	

C W Shipley
Lt Colonel RAMC
Commanding 2/2 W.R. Field Ambulance

ORIGINAL:

62nd Div

Vol 5

Confidential.

War Diary

OF

2/2nd West Riding Field Ambulance,

From 1st May, 1917, to 31st May, 1917.

Volume 5.

COMMITTEE FOR THE
MEDICAL HISTORY OF THE WAR
Date 10 JUL. 1917

Army Form C. 2118.

WAR DIARY
or
INTELLIGENCE SUMMARY.
(Erase heading not required.)

Sheet 1.

Commanding 2/2nd W.R. Field Ambulance.

Place	Date	Hour	Summary of Events and Information	Remarks and references to Appendices
ERVILLERS	1.5.17	—	Two heaver sub-divisions reported for duty with this Unit from the 2/1st West Riding Field Ambulance.	
ERVILLERS	2.5.17	—	Admissions – Officers, Sick Nil, Wounded 1. Other Ranks, Sick 2, Wounded 59.	
ERVILLERS	3.5.17	—	Admissions – Officers, Sick 3, Wounded 23. Other Ranks, Sick 11, Wounded 550.	
ERVILLERS	4.5.17	—	Admissions – Officers, Sick 1, Wounded Nil. Other Ranks, Sick 3, Wounded 73.	
ERVILLERS	5.5.17	—	Admissions – Officers, Sick Nil, Wounded 1. Other Ranks, Sick 2, Wounded 18.	
ERVILLERS	6.5.17	—	Admissions – Officers, Nil. Other Ranks, Sick 1, Wounded 8.	
ERVILLERS	7.5.17	—	Admissions – Officers, Sick Nil, Wounded 1. Other Ranks, Sick 2, Wounded 6.	
ERVILLERS	8.5.17	—	Admissions – Officers, Nil. Other Ranks, Sick Nil, Wounded 2.	
ERVILLERS	9.5.17	—	Admissions – Officers, Sick Nil, Wounded 1. Other Ranks, Sick 2, Wounded 18 (eighteen).	

Army Form C. 2118.

Sheet 2

WAR DIARY
or
INTELLIGENCE SUMMARY
(Erase heading not required.)

~~Commanding~~ 2/2nd W.R. Field Ambulance
~~Lieut-Colonel~~ R.A.M.C.(T)

Place	Date	Hour	Summary of Events and Information	Remarks and references to Appendices
ERVILLERS	10.5.17	GoR	Admissions - Officers NIL. Other Ranks, Sick NIL. Wounded 3	
ERVILLERS	11.5.17	CoR	Admissions - Officers, Sick 1, Wounded NIL. Other Ranks, Sick NIL, Wounded 1.	
ERVILLERS	12.5.17	CoR	Admissions - Officers NIL. Other Ranks, Sick NIL, Wounded 4.	
ERVILLERS	13.5.17	CoR	Admissions - Officers NIL. Other Ranks, Sick 1, Wounded 5.	
ERVILLERS	14.5.17	CoR	Admissions - Officers, Sick 1, Wounded NIL. Other Ranks, Sick 1, Wounded 10.	
ERVILLERS	15.5.17	CoR	Admissions - Officers, Sick 5, Wounded NIL. Other Ranks, Sick 4, Wounded 35.	
ERVILLERS	16.5.17	CoR	Admissions - Officers, Sick 2, Wounded NIL. Other Ranks, Sick NIL, Wounded 5.	
ERVILLERS	17.5.17	CoR	Admissions - Officers, Sick 1, Wounded NIL. Other Ranks, Sick 2, Wounded 2.	
ERVILLERS	18.5.17	CoR	Admissions - Officers NIL. Other Ranks, Sick NIL, Wounded 1.	
ERVILLERS	19.5.17	CoR	Admissions - Officers NIL. Other Ranks, Sick 1, Wounded 4.	
ERVILLERS	20.5.17	CoR	Admissions - Officers, Sick 1, Wounded NIL. Other Ranks, Sick NIL, Wounded 11.	

Sheet 3

Army Form C. 2118.

WAR DIARY
or
INTELLIGENCE SUMMARY.
(Erase heading not required.)

~~Lieut. Colonel, R.A.M.C. (T)~~
~~Commanding 2/2nd W.R. Field Ambulance~~

Instructions regarding War Diaries and Intelligence Summaries are contained in F. S. Regs., Part II. and the Staff Manual respectively. Title pages will be prepared in manuscript.

Place	Date	Hour	Summary of Events and Information	Remarks and references to Appendices
ERVILLERS	21.5.17	a.m.	Admissions - Officers NIL. Other Ranks, Sick 3, Wounded 3.	
ERVILLERS	22.5.17	a.m.	Admissions - Officers NIL. Other Ranks, Sick 2, Wounded 3.	
ERVILLERS	23.5.17	a.m.	Admissions - Officer, Sick NIL, Wounded 1. Other Ranks, Sick NIL, Wounded 8.	
ERVILLERS	24.5.17	a.m.	Admissions - Officers NIL. Other Ranks, Sick 1, Wounded NIL.	
ERVILLERS	25.5.17	a.m.	Admissions - Officers NIL. Other Ranks, Sick NIL, Wounded 1.	
ERVILLERS	26.5.17	a.m.	Admissions - Officers NIL. Other Ranks, Sick NIL, Wounded 5.	
ERVILLERS	27.5.17	a.m.	Admissions - Officers NIL. Other Ranks, Sick NIL, Wounded 9.	
ERVILLERS	28.5.17	a.m.	Admissions - Officers NIL. Other Ranks, Sick NIL, Wounded 4.	
ERVILLERS	29.5.17	a.m.	Admissions - Officers NIL. Other Ranks, Sick NIL, Wounded 2. This Unit was relieved by the 2/3 Home Counties Field Ambulance, and proceeded to BEHAGNIES to take over a hospital for sick.	
BEHAGNIES	30.5.17	a.m.	Admissions - Officers NIL. Other Ranks, Sick 141, Wounded NIL.	
BEHAGNIES	31.5.17	a.m.	Admissions - Officers NIL. Other Ranks, Sick 13, Wounded NIL.	

C. K. Paine
Lieut. Colonel, R.A.M.C. (T)
Commanding 2/2nd W.R. Field Ambulance.

ORIGINAL

Vol 6.

Confidential.

War Diary
of
2/2nd W. R. Field Ambulance.
R.A.M.C. (T)

COMMITTEE FOR THE
MEDICAL HISTORY OF THE WAR
Date — 7 AUG. 1917

From 1st June 1917 to 30th June 1917.

Volume No 6.

WAR DIARY

INTELLIGENCE SUMMARY.

Army Form C. 2118.

(Erase heading not required.)

Instructions regarding War Diaries and Intelligence Summaries are contained in F.S. Regs., Part II. and the Staff Manual respectively. Title pages will be prepared in manuscript.

2/2nd W.R. Field Ambulance, R.A.M.C. (T)

Sheet 1707

ORIGINAL

Place	Date	Hour	Summary of Events and Information	Remarks and references to Appendices
BEHAGNIES	1.6.17	C.WE	General improvements being made to Camp site & surroundings	Appended
BEHAGNIES	2.6.17	C.WE	Strength decreased by one other rank (Sent to base)	Sketch of
BEHAGNIES	3.6.17	C.WE	Capt Seckel R.A.M.C. transferred to Officers Rest Hospital disposition	& Camp &
			5 N.C.O's & 71 men of the unit Granted "First Good Conduct Badge"	surroundings
BEHAGNIES	4.6.17	C.WE	Nothing to report	
BEHAGNIES	5.6.17	C.WE	Nothing to report	
BEHAGNIES	6.6.17	C.WE	Nothing to report	
BEHAGNIES	7.6.17	C.WE	Nothing to report	
BEHAGNIES	8.6.17	C.WE	Lt. Col. C.W. EAMES R.A.M.C. transferred to Officers Rest Hospital Warloy Capt F.W. HIRD R.A.M.C. permanently attached to 2/4 K.O.Y.L.I. is struck off strength	
BEHAGNIES	9.6.17	C.WE	Capt P.H. RAWSON reported for duty from 2/3 W.R. Field Amb. on 8.6.17	
BEHAGNIES	10.6.17	C.WE	10 N.C.O's & men proceed to V'th Corps Summer Rest Camp - ST VALERY SUR SOMME Strength increased by 10 other ranks as reinforcement: A.S.C. 527 Coy. & c Strength increased by 2 other ranks.	
			Average admissions to hospital during first 10 days of month = 15.	

Army Form C. 2118.

WAR DIARY
INTELLIGENCE SUMMARY.
(Erase heading not required.)

Sheet No. 2

2/2nd W.R. Field Ambulance.
R.A.M.C. (T)

Instructions regarding War Diaries and Intelligence Summaries are contained in F.S. Regs., Part II. and the Staff Manual respectively. Title pages will be prepared in manuscript.

Place	Date	Hour	Summary of Events and Information	Remarks and references to Appendices
BEHAGNIES	10.6.17	CWE	60% of cases are diagnosed as P.U.O. which is thought to be consequent	
	(cont.)		upon lice infection. Examination of urine for albumen has been made in	
			each case, with a comparatively negligible result, only being found in	
			3 cases out of a total of 68.	
		CWE	Six cases of Nephritis have been admitted	
BEHAGNIES	11.6.17	CWE	Nothing to report	
BEHAGNIES	12.6.17	CWE	Nothing to report	
BEHAGNIES	13.6.17	CWE	Nothing to report	
BEHAGNIES	14.6.17	CWE	Nothing to report	
BEHAGNIES	15.6.17	CWE	Nothing to report	
BEHAGNIES	16.6.17	CWE	Hospital & Transport inspected by G.O.C 62nd Division	
BEHAGNIES	17.6.17	CWE	Nothing to report	
BEHAGNIES	18.6.17	CWE	Lt. Col. G.B. Eames returned to duty from Officer's Rest Hospital Warley	
BEHAGNIES	19.6.17	CWE	Nothing to report	
BEHAGNIES	20.6.17	CWE	Nothing to report	
BEHAGNIES	21.6.17	CWE	Lieut Jas Shenrick United States Medical Service reported to HQ unit	

Army Form C. 2118.

Sheet No 3

WAR DIARY
INTELLIGENCE SUMMARY.
(Erase heading not required.)

2/2nd W.R. Field Ambulance,
R.A.M.O. (T)

Instructions regarding War Diaries and Intelligence Summaries are contained in F. S. Regs, Part II. and the Staff Manual respectively. Title pages will be prepared in manuscript.

Place	Date	Hour	Summary of Events and Information	Remarks and references to Appendices
BEHAGNIES	21.6.17	CWE (cont)	for duty for instructional purposes	
BEHAGNIES	22.6.17	CWE	Nothing to report	
BEHAGNIES	23.6.17	CWE	Nothing to report	
BEHAGNIES	24.6.17	CWE	Nothing to report	
BEHAGNIES	25.6.17	CWE	Capt Traill Rame reported to 1/4 York Rams for temporary duty – Capt Anderson now complete tent Sub-Division reported to O.C. No 9 C.C.S. AVELUY for temp'y duty	
BEHAGNIES	26.6.17	CWE	Capt A.W Sickel Rame being evacuated to Base is struck off the strength	
BEHAGNIES	27.6.17	CWE	Took over charge of V th Corps Scabies Hospital at Bucquoy Field Achiet-le-Grand Map Ref. 57C G.9 b 7.1 from 2/1st HC of Ambce	
ACHIET-LE GRAND	28.6.17	CWE	Nothing to report 27.6.17 Two bearer Sub-Divisions + one tent Sub-Division under Capt Darce reported to 2/3 W.R. Fd Ambce for temp'y duty	
ACHIET LE GRAND	29.6.17	CWE	Nothing to report.	
ACHIET-LE GRAND	30.6.17	CWE	Nothing to report.	

C.K Rame
Lieut. Colonel, R.A.M.O.(T)
Commanding 2/2nd W.R. Field Ambulance

John R Kennewby
Capt Rame
for O.C.
2/2 West Riding Fd Ambce
30/6/17

2/2nd W.R. Field Ambulance
R.A.M.C. (T)

461 Coy R.E.'s in Bivouacs.

MAP REFERENCE
57 C. H.I. d 8·3

Main ARRAS – BAPAUME Road

CART TRACK

RAMC Personel.

SERGEANTS

Incinerator

HEDGE 10' high

Latrine

OFFICERS LINES

Mess for Personel

Stores

Rack Stores Joiner   Trench Line
                       Cook House   Map Safe
                       Ablution Bench   P.T.

HEDGE 10' high

Boschè Barbed Wire

PARADE GROUND

LATRINES
Personel Patients
oooooooo oooooo

Drying Room
Bath
Mob. Stores
Salvage

A+D tent

Diarrhoea Medical Surgical Dispensary ORDERLY ROOM

Brick Path

IN OUT

✛

Motor Transport

Forage Stores – Farrier

Wagon Lines

Horse Lines

Transport Personel

N ↑ S ↓

BEHAGNIES — BIHUCOURT ROAD

30th M.A.C.

D. Kenworthy
C. W. Cannon
Capt RAMC

ORIGINAL

Confidential.

War Diary.
of
2/2 W. R. Field Amb:ce

from 1 July to 31 July 1917

Volume 7

COMMITTEE FOR THE
MEDICAL HISTORY OF THE WAR
Date 10 SEP.1917

Army Form C. 2118.

WAR DIARY
INTELLIGENCE SUMMARY.
(Erase heading not required.)

2/2nd W. R. Field Ambulance

ORIGINAL

Place	Date	Hour	Summary of Events and Information	Remarks and references to Appendices
ACHIET-LE-GRAND	1.7.16		Map Reference 57 C. G.9. 67.1. The unit is still in charge of the VIth Corps Scabies Hospital combined with Field Hospital	Appended DRK Sketch of
ACHIET-LE-GRAND	2.7.16		Nothing to report	DRK Disposition
ACHIET-LE-GRAND	3.7.16		Do	DRK of Camp &
ACHIET-LE-GRAND	4.7.16		Do	DRK Surroundings
ACHIET-LE-GRAND	5.7.16		Capt G. M. Verers France reported to this unit for duty on 4.7.16	DRK
ACHIET-LE-GRAND	6.7.16		The Tent Sub-Division temporarily attached to the 2/3 WR Field Ambce returned from that unit reported to the Vth Corps Rest Station for Temp. July	DRK
ACHIET-LE-GRAND	7.7.16		The Vth Corps having moved out they replaced by the VIth Corps. This station is now known as the "VIth Corps Scabies Hospital"	DRK
ACHIET-LE-GRAND	8.7.16		Nothing to report	DRK
ACHIET-LE-GRAND	9.7.16		Capt Trail RAMC returned to this unit from Temp. July attc to 2/4 York Lancs.	DRK
ACHIET-LE-GRAND	10.7.16		Nothing to report	DRK
ACHIET-LE-GRAND	11.7.16		Do	DRK

Army Form C. 2118.

WAR DIARY

INTELLIGENCE SUMMARY.
(Erase heading not required.)

2/2nd W. R. Field Ambulance

Instructions regarding War Diaries and Intelligence Summaries are contained in F. S. Regs., Part II. and the Staff Manual respectively. Title pages will be prepared in manuscript.

Place	Date	Hour	Summary of Events and Information	Remarks and references to Appendices
ACHIET-LE-GRAND	12.7.17		Nothing to report	OCK
ACHIET-LE-GRAND	13.7.17		Do	OCK
ACHIET-LE-GRAND	14.7.17		During the first 14 days of July 28 cases diagnosed as P.U.O. were admitted to this hospital. The urine was examined in each case for albumen with a negative result throughout	OCK
ACHIET-LE-GRAND	15.7.17		Nothing to report	OCK
ACHIET-LE-GRAND	16.7.17		Nothing to report	OCK
ACHIET-LE-GRAND	17.7.17		15 other ranks returned to this unit for duty, from temporary duty with 2/3 W.R. Field Ambulance	OCK
ACHIET-LE-GRAND	18.7.17		Nothing to report	OCK
ACHIET-LE-GRAND	19.7.17		Nothing to report	OCK
ACHIET-LE-GRAND	20.7.17		Nothing to report	OCK
ACHIET-LE-GRAND	21.7.17		One N.C.O. + 14 men reported to 1st Major from FAVREUIL for temporary duty for Sanitating	OCK
ACHIET-LE-GRAND	22.7.17		Nothing to report	OCK

Army Form C. 2118.

WAR DIARY

INTELLIGENCE SUMMARY.
(Erase heading not required.)

2/2nd W.R. Field Ambulance

Instructions regarding War Diaries and Intelligence Summaries are contained in F.S. Regs., Part II. and the Staff Manual respectively. Title pages will be prepared in manuscript.

Place	Date	Hour	Summary of Events and Information	Remarks and references to Appendices
ACHIET-LE-GRAND	23.7.17		Nothing to report	DCh.
ACHIET-LE-GRAND	24.7.17		Capt. R. Traill RAMC proceeded to Paris Plage. Capt. A. M. Davie RAMC proceeded to 1/4 Duke of Wellington's Regt for temporary duty as Medical Officer. Lt-Col E.W. Eames RAMC granted 10 days leave to England; Capt. A.G. Debble Mustante RAMC took over command of this unit	DCh.
ACHIET-LE-GRAND	25.7.17		Nothing to report	DCh.
ACHIET-LE-GRAND	26.7.17		Nothing to report	DCh.
ACHIET-LE-GRAND	27.7.17		Nothing to report	DCh.
ACHIET-LE-GRAND	28.7.17		Nothing to report	DCh.
ACHIET-LE-GRAND	29.7.17		Nothing to report	DCh.
ACHIET-LE-GRAND	30.7.17		Inspection of V Corps Scabies Station by General Stockwell G.O.C. V Corps. Also expressed complete satisfaction. A/S/Sergt Major R. Cooke (527 Coy ASC attd) was reverted to rank of Sergt by authority of 11th Corps. Proceeding to report to O.C. 62nd Divisional Train. Is struck off Strength accordingly	DCh.

Army Form C. 2118.

WAR DIARY
or
INTELLIGENCE SUMMARY.

2/2nd W. R. Field Ambulance

(Erase heading not required.)

Instructions regarding War Diaries and Intelligence Summaries are contained in F. S. Regs., Part II. and the Staff Manual respectively. Title pages will be prepared in manuscript.

Place	Date	Hour	Summary of Events and Information	Remarks and references to Appendices
ACHIET-LE-GRAND	31.7.17	AM	Since 14.7.17, 13 cases of "P.U.O." have been admitted. In one case was albuminuria found. Capt A Irvine RAMC returned from six days' leave at Paris Plage.	

AMilliount
CAPTAIN. R.A.M.C. (T.)
for Lieut. Colonel, R.A.M.C.(T).
Commanding 2/2nd W. R. Field Ambulance.

John R Kennedy Capt
RAMC T
OC 2/2 West Riding
Field Ambulance
31.7.17

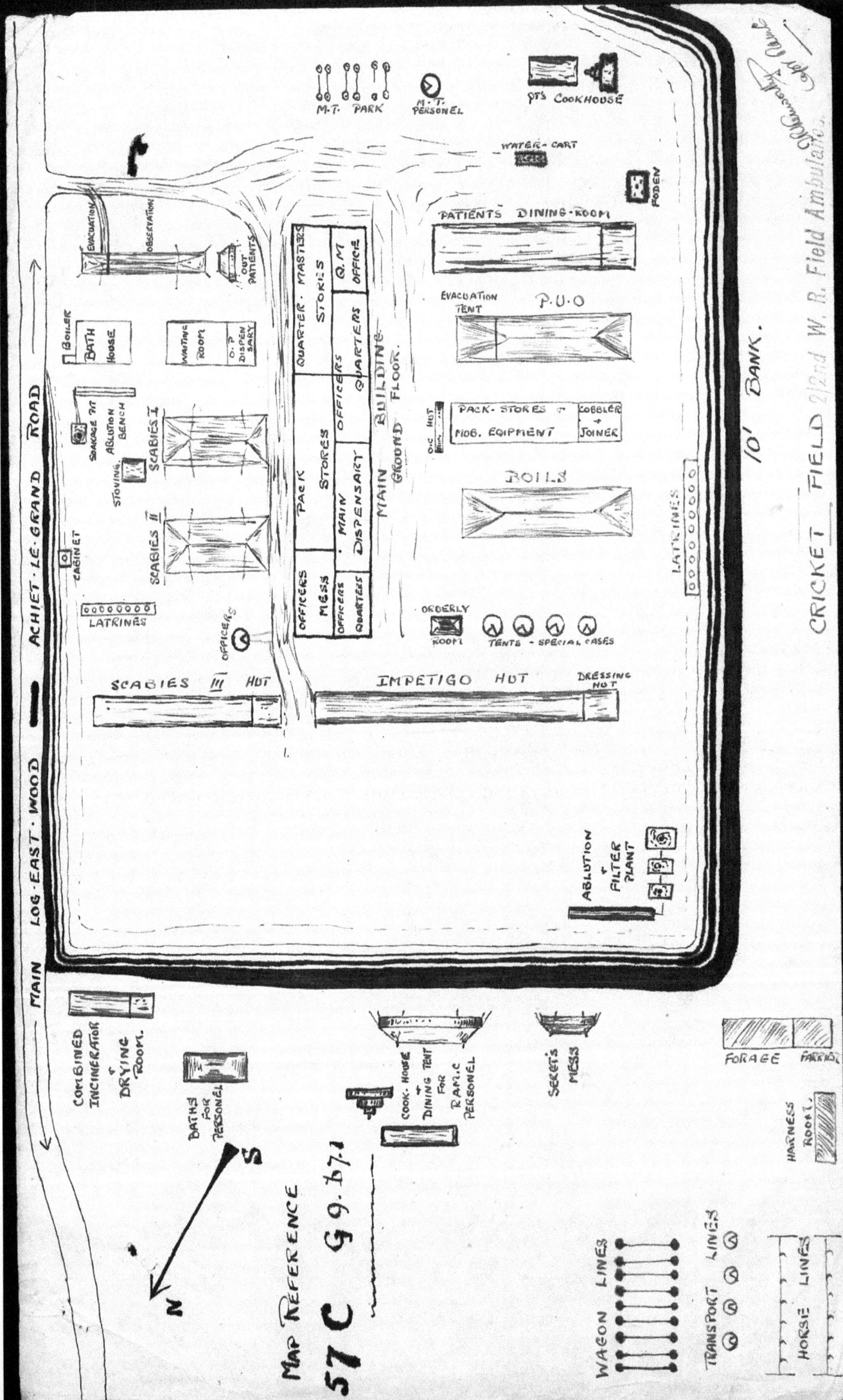

ORIGINAL

Aug 1917

140/2364

Vol 8

CONFIDENTIAL

COMMITTEE FOR THE
MEDICAL HISTORY OF THE WAR
Date -1 OCT. 1917

War Diary
of
2/2nd W. R. Field Ambulance,
R.A.M.C. (T)

From 1st Aug: 1917 to 31st Aug: 1917.

Volume 8.

Army Form C. 2118.

212nd W.R. Field Ambulance,
R.A.M.C. (T)

WAR DIARY
INTELLIGENCE SUMMARY.
(Erase heading not required.)

ORIGINAL

Place	Date	Hour	Summary of Events and Information	Remarks and references to Appendices
ACHIET-LE-GRAND	1.6.17		Map Reference 57 C G.9 b.7.1 The unit is still in charge of 115 W.R Corps Scabies Hospital & Field Hospital	226
ACHIET-LE-GRAND	2.6.17		Nothing to report	226
ACHIET-LE-GRAND	3.6.17		200 leary-draughts taken on strength as reinforcements	226
ACHIET-LE-GRAND	4.6.17		Nothing to report	226
ACHIET-LE-GRAND	5.6.17		Lt-Col C.B. Eames returned from 10 days leave to England, Capt. Alf. Stebblethwaite relinquishing temporary command	226
ACHIET-LE-GRAND	6.6.17		Nothing to report	226
ACHIET-LE-GRAND	7.6.17		Nothing to report	226
ACHIET-LE-GRAND	8.6.17		Nothing to report	226
ACHIET-LE-GRAND	9.6.17		The unit took over charge of VIth Corps Rest Station from the 23rd Field Ambce. Map Reference 57 C G.9 c.6.2. 4 N.C.O's & 33 O.R. returned from temporary duty with 2/3 W.R. Field Ambce.	226
ACHIET-LE-GRAND	10.6.17		2 Officers 19 N.C.O's & O.R. are attached for temporary duty	226
ACHIET-LE-GRAND	11.6.17		Nothing to report	226

Army Form C. 2118.

WAR DIARY
INTELLIGENCE SUMMARY.
(Erase heading not required.)

2/2nd W.R. Field Ambulance
R.A.M.C. (T)

Place	Date	Hour	Summary of Events and Information	Remarks and references to Appendices
ACHIET-LE-GRAND	12/8/17		2 Officers 19 NCO's +OR. Temporarily attached from 2/3rd Field Ambce returned to Duty with their own unit.	
ACHIET-LE-GRAND	13/8/17		1 NCO +7H OR. temporarily attached to Town Major BUCQUOY as hay making party returned to this unit for duty. Nothing to report	2CA 2CA
ACHIET-LE-GRAND	14/8/17		Capt'n A Traill RAMC TC reported to OC 2/4 West Riding Fd Ambce as permanent MO vis struck off strength accordingly for duty	2CA 2CA
ACHIET-LE-GRAND	15/8/17		Nothing to report	2CA
ACHIET-LE-GRAND	16/8/17		Do	2CA
ACHIET-LE-GRAND	17/8/17		Do	2CA
ACHIET-LE-GRAND	18/8/17		Do	2CA
ACHIET-LE-GRAND	19/8/17		1 NCO +19 OR. proceeded to report to OC 13th CCS Tincourt for temporary duty	2CA
ACHIET-LE-GRAND	20/8/17		Nothing to report	2CA
ACHIET-LE-GRAND	21/8/17		Do	2CA
ACHIET-LE-GRAND	22/8/17		Do	2CA

Army Form C. 2118.

WAR DIARY
INTELLIGENCE SUMMARY.
(Erase heading not required.)

2/2nd W.R. Field Ambulance
R.A.M.C. (T)

Place	Date	Hour	Summary of Events and Information	Remarks and references to Appendices
ACHIET-LE-GRAND	23/8/17		Nothing to report	22h
ACHIET-LE-GRAND	24/8/17		1 N.C.O. & 19 O.R. returned from temporary duty at No 13 D.B.S. Capt A. McDavie R.A.M.C.T. reported to O.C. 2/1st West Riding Regt as temporary M.O.	22h
ACHIET-LE-GRAND	25/8/17		Nothing to report	22h
ACHIET-LE-GRAND	26/8/17		Nothing to report	22h
ACHIET-LE-GRAND	27/8/17		Capt J.R. Gibson R.A.M.C. reported to this unit for duty & is taken on strength accordingly. (late 56 Labour Group)	22h
ACHIET-LE-GRAND	28/8/17		Nothing to report	22h
ACHIET-LE-GRAND	29/8/17		Nothing to report	22h
ACHIET-LE-GRAND	30/8/17		Capt H.O. Smith R.A.M.C.T.C. (from 20th Reserve Park) reported to this unit for temporary duty (orders:- DDMS VIth Corps)	22h
ACHIET-LE-GRAND	31/8/17		Capt Alf. Heslop Iswaite R.A.M.C.T. was attached to DADMS 11th Corps on 28/6/17 & as accordingly struck off the strength of this unit.	22h

C.W. Paris
Lieut. Colonel, R.A.M.C.(T)
Commanding 2/2nd W.R. Field Ambulance

Don R. Kensworthy
C.W. Paris
Lieut Colonel
O.C. 2/2 West Riding Field Ambulance

ORIGINAL CONFIDENTIAL

War Diary

of

2/2nd W. R. Field Ambulance.

from Sept 1st 1917 to Sept 30th 1917

Volume 9

COMMITTEE FOR THE
MEDICAL HISTORY OF THE WAR
Date -5 NOV.1917

Army Form C. 2118.

WAR DIARY
INTELLIGENCE SUMMARY

2/2nd W.R. Field Ambulance.

Sheet 1.

ORIGINAL

Place	Date	Hour	Summary of Events and Information	Remarks and references to Appendices
ACHIET-LE-GRAND	1.9.17		The unit is still in charge of the 11th Corps Rest Station. Map Ref. 57.C.G.9.c.6.2. Lieut Jn Sterich U.S.M.C. detailed to attend Senior Officer's course at Divisional Gas School	
ACHIET-LE-GRAND	2.9.17		Six other ranks proceeded to 11th Corps Rest Camp Valery sur Somme for a period of 14 days.	
ACHIET-LE-GRAND	3.9.17		Six NCO's + 11 O.R reported to No 9 CCS to replace 5 NCO's + 12 O.R who reported for duty. Capt. J.R. Wilson RAMC T.C reported to O.C 56 Labour Co for temporary duty.	
ACHIET-LE-GRAND	4.9.17		Nothing to report	
ACHIET-LE-GRAND	5.9.17			
ACHIET-LE-GRAND	6.9.17		Capt H.O Smith RAMC T.C reported to DDMS 11th Corps + cease to be attached to this unit from 5.9.17. Capt J.R. Wilson RAMC T.C reported back to this unit from temporary duty with 56 Labour Co.	
ACHIET-LE-GRAND	7.9.17		2.O.C + Ten 527 G. A.S.C reported as reinforcements + ten taken on the strength. NINE ASC batmen were returned to	

Army Form C. 2118.

WAR DIARY
INTELLIGENCE SUMMARY.
(Erase heading not required.)

2/2nd W.R. Field Ambulance

Sheet 2

Place	Date	Hour	Summary of Events and Information	Remarks and references to Appendices
ACHIET-LE-GRAND	7.9.17		(CONT.) O.C. H.T. & S. Base Depôt Havre on instructions of GHQ 3rd Echelon (No.O/140 6/3) are struck off the strength. 10 O.R.B. batmen reported for duty in their place. Have taken on nil strength.	O.C.H.
ACHIET-LE-GRAND	8.9.17		Nothing to report	O.C.H.
ACHIET-LE-GRAND	9.9.17		Do	O.C.H.
ACHIET-LE-GRAND	10.9.17		One other A.S.C. batman returned to O.C. H.T. & S. Base Depôt Havre. Lieut. Col. G.N.Eames took over temp. duty of A.D.M.S.	O.C.H.
ACHIET-LE-GRAND	11.9.17		Nothing to report	O.C.H.
ACHIET-LE-GRAND	12.9.17		do	O.C.H.
ACHIET-LE-GRAND	13.9.17		do	O.C.H.
ACHIET-LE-GRAND	14.9.17		do	O.C.H.
ACHIET-LE-GRAND	15.9.17		Six O.R. proceeded to 3rd Army Rest Camp St Valery sur Somme for 14 days	O.C.H.
ACHIET-LE-GRAND	16.9.17		Nothing to report	O.C.H.
ACHIET-LE-GRAND	17.9.17		Nothing to report	O.C.H.

Army Form C. 2118.

WAR DIARY
INTELLIGENCE SUMMARY
(Erase heading not required.)

2/2nd W.R. Field Ambulance

Place	Date	Hour	Summary of Events and Information	Remarks and references to Appendices
ACHIET-LE-GRAND	18.9.17		Nothing to report	DRK
ACHIET-LE-GRAND	19.9.17		Do	DRK
ACHIET-LE-GRAND	20.9.17		Capt J.R. Wilson RAMC T.C. reported for duty as Batt. M.O. to 2/6 West Riding and struck off strength accordingly.	DRK
ACHIET-LE-GRAND	21.9.17		Nothing to report	DRK
ACHIET-LE-GRAND	22.9.17		Do	DRK
ACHIET-LE-GRAND	23.9.17		Do	DRK
ACHIET-LE-GRAND	24.9.17		Do	DRK
ACHIET-LE-GRAND	25.9.17		Do	DRK
ACHIET-LE-GRAND	26.9.17		Do	SRK
ACHIET-LE-GRAND	27.9.17		Lieut Puntnell proceeded to III Army School of Cooking 23.9.17 returned 27/9/17.	AWP
-do-	28.9.17		Nothing to report	CWP
-do-	29.9.17		Nothing to report	CWP
-do-	30.9.17		Nothing to report	CWP

J.K. Rames
Lieut. Colonel, R.A.M.C.(T)
Commanding. 2/2nd W.R. Field Ambulance.

ORIGINAL

Confidential Vol 10

40/2499

War Diary

of

2/2nd West Riding Field Ambulance,
R.A.M.C. (T)

COMMITTEE FOR THE
MEDICAL HISTORY OF THE WAR
Date 8 DEC. 1917

from 1st Oct: 1917 to 31st Oct: 1917.

Volume 10.

"MEDICAL"

Army Form C. 2118.

2/2nd West Riding Field Ambulance,
R.A.M.C. (T)

WAR DIARY

INTELLIGENCE SUMMARY.

(Erase heading not required.)

ORIGINAL

Place	Date	Hour	Summary of Events and Information	Remarks and references to Appendices
ACHIET-LE-GRAND	1.10.17		The unit is still in command of the VIth Corps REST STATION SOUTH erecting the new site at BIHUCOURT	JCR
ACHIET-LE-GRAND	2.10.17		CAPT DAVIE A.M. RAMC T reported from 2/4 WRFR for temporary duty. CAPT VEVERS G.M. RAMC T.C. reported to O.C. V CORPS SCHOOL VAUCHELLES Yrs struck off Strength from this day	JCR
			CAPT WALKER C.D. RAMC TC reported for duty. His taken on strength accordingly. CAPT KENWORTH returned from Paris leave	JCR
ACHIET-LE-GRAND	3.10.17		Nothing to report	JCR
ACHIET-LE-GRAND	4.10.17		Do	JCR
ACHIET-LE-GRAND	5.10.17		Do	JCR
ACHIET-LE-GRAND	6.10.17		CAPT DANE A M RAMC T returned to 2/4 WRFR from Temp duty	JCR
ACHIET-LE-GRAND	7.10.17		CAPT WALKER C.D. RAMC TC reported for duty to 61 LABOUR GROUP as struck off strength accordingly	JCR
ACHIET-LE-GRAND	8.10.17		Nothing to report	JCR
ACHIET-LE-GRAND	9.10.17		2 NCO's + 18 O.R. proceeded to report to TOWN MAJOR FAVREUIL for temporary duty	JCR

Army Form C. 2118.

WAR DIARY
INTELLIGENCE SUMMARY.

2/2nd West Riding Field Ambulance
R.A.M.C. (T)

(Erase heading not required.)

Place	Date	Hour	Summary of Events and Information	Remarks and references to Appendices
ACHIET-LE-GRAND	11.10.17		G.O.C 62nd Division inspected the unit. The new S/c for VI CORPS REST STATION at BIHUCOURT expressed his satisfaction. CAPT KENWORTHY RAMC 4 NCO's 21 OR proceed as advance party to BEAULENCOURT as advance party.	2Ok.
ACHIET-LE-GRAND	12.10.17		VI CORPS REST STATION SOUTH handed over to 8th Field Ambulance. The unit marched to BEAULENCOURT opened a Field Hospital Chaplovay Oll.	
BEAULENCOURT	13.10.17		Nothing to report	2Ok
BEAULENCOURT	14.10.17		2 NCO's 16 OR reported from TOWN MAJOR FAVREUIL	2Ok
BEAULENCOURT	15.10.17		CAPT MARTIN G.E. RAMC T. reported for temp duty vice taken on strength accordingly CAPT ANDERSON RAMC 4 NCO's 14 OR reported from temporary duty with No 9 CCS AVELUOY	2Ok
BEAULENCOURT	16.10.17		Nothing to report	2Ok
BEAULENCOURT	17.10.17		Do	2Ok
BEAULENCOURT	18.10.17		Do	2Ok
BEAULENCOURT	19.10.17		Do	2Ok
LE TRANSLOY	20.10.17		The unit move to LE TRANSLOY reopens Rest Hospital	2Ok

T2134. Wt. W708—776. 500000. 4/15. Sir J. C. & S.

Army Form C. 2118.

WAR DIARY
INTELLIGENCE SUMMARY.
(Erase heading not required.)

2/2nd West Riding Field Ambulance
R.A.M.C. (T)

Instructions regarding War Diaries and Intelligence Summaries are contained in F. S. Regs., Part II. and the Staff Manual respectively. Title pages will be prepared in manuscript.

Place	Date	Hour	Summary of Events and Information	Remarks and references to Appendices
LE TRANSLOY	21.10.17		CAPT ANDERSON R.A.M.C. proceeded on 10 days leave to ENGLAND	DRK
LE TRANSLOY	22.10.17		Nothing to report	DRK
LE TRANSLOY	23.10.17		Nothing to report	DRK
LE TRANSLOY	24.10.17		Nothing to report	DRK
LE TRANSLOY	25.10.17		The D.D.M.S. (IV CORPS) inspected the camp & expressed satisfaction on the way the work was being carried out	DRK
LE TRANSLOY	26.10.17		Nothing to report	DRK
LE TRANSLOY	27.10.17		Do	DRK
LE TRANSLOY	28.10.17		4 Riders (surplus to establishment) were transferred to DDR III ARMY taken off strength accordingly	DRK
LE TRANSLOY	29.10.17		Nothing to report	DRK
LE TRANSLOY	30.10.17		This unit handed over the camp to AREA COMMANDANT & proceeded to GOMIECOURT village & bivouaced for the night at point A.23 d 1.3 Sheet 57 C N.W.	DRK
LE TRANSLOY	31.10.17		CAPT AMT HALLIGAN R.a.m.C T.C., CAPT ST BRENNAN R.a.m.C T.C., CAPT NEILANY A.T. reported for permanent duty & are later on the	

Army Form C. 2118.

WAR DIARY
INTELLIGENCE SUMMARY
(Erase heading not required.)

2/2nd West Riding Field Ambulance
R.A.M.C. (T)

Instructions regarding War Diaries and Intelligence Summaries are contained in F.S. Regs., Part II. and the Staff Manual respectively. Title pages will be prepared in manuscript.

Place	Date	Hour	Summary of Events and Information	Remarks and references to Appendices
LE TRANSLOY	31.10.17		Strength accordingly. The unit handed over the temporary quarters at GOMIECOURT (Sheet 57 C A.23 d.13) to Town Major & proceeded to GOUY EN ARTOIS taking over quarters at point (Sheet 57 C P.18 d.16) on 3.30 p.m. A full Dilution Hospital was opened immediately on taking over the new site. J.K.	

C.W.Sam.
Lieut. Colonel R.A.M.C.(T)
Commanding 2/2nd W.R. Field Ambulance.

J.Kennerly
Captain R.A.M.C.(T)
for Lt. Colonel R.A.M.C.(T) O.C.
2/2 West Riding Field Ambulance
31.10.17

"MEDICAL"

ORIGINAL

CONFIDENTIAL.

WAR DIARY

of

2/2nd WEST RIDING FIELD AMBULANCE.

From 1st Novr. 1917 to 30th Novr. 1917.

VOLUME No: 11.

COMMITTEE FOR THE
MEDICAL HISTORY OF THE WAR
Date 17 JAN. 1918

MEDICAL.

Army Form C. 2118.

WAR DIARY
or
INTELLIGENCE SUMMARY.
(Erase heading not required.)

Summary of Events and Information 2/2nd W.R. Field Ambulance

Place	Date	Hour	Summary of Events and Information	Remarks and references to Appendices
GOUY	1.11.17		The unit is running the Group Field Ambulance & also 62nd Divisional	Sheet 57C
			Rest Station	P15. S.1.6
GOUY	2.11.17		Nothing to report	JCk
GOUY	3.11.17		Do	JCk
GOUY	4.11.17		49001 a/S/M Earle W trans ferred to No 8 CCS & is struck off	JCk
			strength T4/244223 S/S/M T Thompson reported for duty &	
			is taken on strength – also 10 RAMC reinforcements	JCk
GOUY	5.11.17		Nothing to report	JCk
GOUY	6.11.17		Do	JCk
GOUY	7.11.17		Do	JCk
GOUY	8.11.17		Capt G.E. MARTIN RAMC T. reported for duty to No 10 CCS is	JCk
			taken off strength accordingly	
GOUY	9.11.17		Nothing to report	JCk
GOUY	10.11.17		Do	JCk
GOUY	11.11.17		Do	JCk
GOUY	12.11.17		Do	JCk

Army Form C. 2118.

WAR DIARY
INTELLIGENCE SUMMARY.
(Erase heading not required.)

2/2nd W. R. Field Ambulance

Place	Date	Hour	Summary of Events and Information	Remarks and references to Appendices
COUY	13.11.17		Nothing to report	JRh
COUY	14.11.17		Camp site landed over & Unit marched out to ACHIET-LE-GRAND Sheet 57C G.9.b.2.6. Opening Detention Hospital for sick immediately on arrival.	JRh
ACHIET-LE-GRAND	15.11.17		Camp site rented over unit proceeded to take over site of M.D. Field Ambulance O.23.C.5.2	JRh
BUS	16.11.17		Nothing to report	JRh
BUS	17.11.17		Nothing to report	JRh
BUS	18.11.17		Lieut Hutchinson (M.O i/c 312 Bde R.F.A.) reported to this unit for duty vice re-attached to 21 B.B.S.	JRh
BUS	18.11.17		16.21 B.B.S. to 312 R.F.A. & Capt A.T. Neilan RAMC T.C. reported to 312 & 240 R. proceeded accordingly. Shoot off shingle 3 NCO's & 24 O.R. proceeded to 21 CCS YPRES for temporary duty	JRh
BUS	19.11.17		Nothing to report	JRh
BUS	20.11.17		Capt T. KENWORTHY RamCT. 6 NCO's & 68 O.R. reported to O.C 2/3 W.R.F. Amb. for temporary duty; also 3 motor amb.	JRh

Army Form C. 2118.

WAR DIARY
INTELLIGENCE SUMMARY
(Erase heading not required.)

2/2nd W. R. Field Ambulance

Place	Date	Hour	Summary of Events and Information	Remarks and references to Appendices
BUS	20.11.17		4 cars, Mess servis, Mess orderlies not 2 H.D. ambulances, One G.S. report, 2 limber G.S., 16 H.D. horses, 4 Mules, 1 Rider & H.T. turned in same. Capt D. Bell RAMC re- posted for temporary duty. 75502 Pte Gamilees of this unit wounded also 110344 Pte J.N. Barker Pte Welsh killed in action & buried near Inniencourt Wood 57 C J 36 a.o.6. Temp Sergt M.A.Endacott reported for duty & taken on strength.	ack.
BUS	21.11.17		The unit is running the Corps Walking Wounded Dressing Station	ack.
BUS	22.11.17		During the battle for CAMBRAI	ack.
BUS	23.11.17		Nothing to report	ack.
BUS	24.11.17		Capt T.D.Bell returned to 62 D.A.C. from temp. duty	ack.
BUS	25.11.17		Nothing to report	ack.
BUS	26.11.17		Do	ack.
BUS	27.11.17		Do	ack.
BUS	28.11.17		Do	ack.

Army Form C. 2118.

WAR DIARY
INTELLIGENCE SUMMARY.
(Erase heading not required.)

Instructions regarding War Diaries and Intelligence Summaries are contained in F. S. Regs., Part II. and the Staff Manual respectively. Title pages will be prepared in manuscript.

Summary of Events and Information 2/2nd W. R. Field Ambulance

Place	Date	Hour	Summary of Events and Information	Remarks and references to Appendices
BUS	29/11/17		2 NCO's & 19 OR of HT & MT awarded First Good Conduct Badges.	20h
BUS	30/11/17		Capt T R Kenworthy RAMC T. & 403463 Pte Styan H O both slightly wounded — remained on duty. Capt T R Kenworthy 14 NCO's 73 OR with 1 Rider 12 HD horses 6 Mules & HT & MT Personnel returned from temporary duty with 2/3 WR Fd Ambce Lieut J W Slemick MC USA reported to O C 2/5 Duke Wellin^s Regt for duty as M.O. 2/c & is accordingly struck off the Strength	20h

O R Kenworthy
Capt RAMC T.
For Lieut Colonel
O/C 2/2 West Riding Field Ambce

G Kinne
Lieut. Colonel, R.A.M.C.(T)
Commanding 2/2nd W.R. Field Ambulance

140/267

2/1st West Riding F.A.

COMMITTEE FOR THE
MEDICAL HISTORY OF THE WAR
Date —1 FEB. 1918

"MEDICAL"

Army Form C.
Vol 1? Sheet 1

WAR DIARY
or
INTELLIGENCE SUMMARY.
(Erase heading not required.)

Instructions regarding War Diaries and Intelligence Summaries are contained in F.S. Regs., Part II. and the Staff Manual respectively. Title pages will be prepared in manuscript.

2/2nd W.R. Field Ambulance.

ORIGINAL

Place	Date	Hour	Summary of Events and Information	Remarks and references to Appendices
BUS.	1/12/17		The Unit is running the Corps walking wounded Station for the battle in front of CAMBRAI.	do
			Temp.t Sgt Major A. ENDACOTT proceeded to WOOLWICH to report to the A.D.M.S. there upon being appointed Temp. Quartermaster R.A.M.C. & was struck off the strength of the unit accordingly	do
BUS	2.12.17		3 N.C.O.'s & 29 O.R's proceeded to the A.D.S. HAVRINCOURT. (47.th DIVISION) for temporary duty. 403528 Act 2/Cpl F WATKINSON was slightly wounded	do
BUS	3.12.17		3 NCO's & 29 OR's returned to the unit from temporary duty with the 47.th DIVISION.	do
			The Unit handed over the site occupied at BUS to the 6.th LONDON FIELD AMBULANCE	do
BAILLEULMONT	4.12.17		The Unit proceeded from BUS to BAILLEULMONT, the Horse & Motor Transport the whole way by road, the rest of the Unit marched from BUS to FREMICOURT where they entrained to BEAUMETZ, them proceeding the remainder of the way to BAILLEULMONT on foot.	do

Army Form C. 2118.

Sheet 2

WAR DIARY
or
INTELLIGENCE SUMMARY.
(Erase heading not required.)

2/2nd W.R. Field Ambulance

Place	Date	Hour	Summary of Events and Information	Remarks and references to Appendices
BAILLEULMONT	4.12.17		The unit immediately upon arrival spend a small Field Amb Hospital. The unit was quartered for the night in billets	do
MONTENESCOURT	5.12.17		The billets at BAILLEULMONT were handed over to the TOWN MAJOR & the Unit proceeded by road to MONTENESCOURT where they were billeted for the night	do
			LIEUT HUTCHINSON, 3 NCO's & 24 OR's returned to the Unit from temporary duty with the 21.C.C.S at YTRES	do
BERLES.	6.12.17.		The billets were handed over the billets at MONTENESCOURT & proceeded by road to BERLES where the unit was quartered in billets	do
BERLES	7.12.17		Nothing to Report.	do
BERLES	8.12.17		Capt E.C. LANG. RAMC(R) D.S.O reported to the unit for duty in return with strength 3 NCO's & 21 OR's comprising a portion of the Divisional Bands & T.O men left this unit & returned to 62nd DIVISIONAL H.Qrs having been attached to this unit as additional help whilst the unit was running the Corps. walking wounded station at BUS.	do
BERLES	9.12.17		Nothing to Report.	do

Army Form C. 2118.

Sheet 3

WAR DIARY
or
INTELLIGENCE SUMMARY.
(Erase heading not required.)

Instructions regarding War Diaries and Intelligence Summaries are contained in F. S. Regs., Part II. and the Staff Manual respectively. Title pages will be prepared in manuscript.

2/2nd W.R. Field Ambulance.

Place	Date	Hour	Summary of Events and Information	Remarks and references to Appendices
ANNEZIN	10.12.17		The Unit landed in the billet at BERLES & proceeded by road to ANNEZIN where the unit was quartered in billets. A small temporary Field Hospital was opened upon arrival, to deal with the Brigade Sick.	
ANNEZIN	11.12.17		Nothing to report.	
ANNEZIN	12.12.17		Do	
ANNEZIN	13.12.17		Do	
ANNEZIN & GONNEHEM	14.12.17		The Unit landed over the billets at ANNEZIN & proceeded to GONNEHEM where quarters were secured in billets, a small temporary Field Hospital being opened upon arrival, to deal with the Brigade Sick who were collected & transferred to C.R.S. & C.C.S. the same day. T4/253991 Sgt J.TATE (A.S.C. H.T. attd) proceeded to the 12th VETERINARY COURSE held at the 14. VETERINARY HOSPITAL. ABBEVILLE	
GONNEHEM	15.12.17		The D.R.O. of today dated announced that "Military Medals" have been awarded to 403567 a/L/C J HILLERBY & 403249 Pte G.T PEAKMAN respectively for gallantry during the operations which commenced on NOV 20th 1917.	

Army Form C. 2118.

WAR DIARY
or
INTELLIGENCE SUMMARY.
(Erase heading not required.)

2/2nd W. R. Field Ambulance. Sheet 4

Place	Date	Hour	Summary of Events and Information	Remarks and references to Appendices
GONNEHEM	16 XII 17		CAPT S.J. BRENNAN proceeded to the 2/5 YORK & LANCS for temporary duty as M.O. CAPT A.M.J. HALLIGAN reported to the O.C. 1st CORPS REINFORCEMENT CAMP ALLOUAGNE, for the examination of reinforcements to this Division & returned to this Unit for duty the same day	aa
GONNEHEM	17 XII 17		LIEUT HUTCHINSON reported to the 2/6 WEST RIDING REGT for temporary duty as M.O.	aa
GONNEHEM / ANNEZIN	18 XII 17		CAPT T.R KENWORTHY was admitted into the No 1 C.C.S. CHOCQUES and removed from the strength of this Unit. The Unit Paraded and the Entered GONNEHEM & proceeded by road to ANNEZIN where they took over the same billets as occupied formerly	aa
BETHENCOURT	19 XII 17		The Unit Paraded and the billets at ANNEZIN to the Town Major & proceeded by road to BETHENCOURT where billets were taken over	aa
BETHENCOURT	20 XII 17		Nothing to Report	aa
BETHENCOURT	21 XII 17		Six NCO's & 13 O.R's reported to the XIII CORPS REST STATION AUBIGNY for temporary duty	aa
BETHENCOURT	22 XII 17		403096 L/C. E. HARRISON reported to the XIII CORPS REINFORCEMENT CAMP for temporary duty as M.O.'s Orderly	aa

T2134. Wt. W708-776. 500000. 4/15. Sir J. C. & S.

Army Form C. 2118
Sheet 5

WAR DIARY
or
INTELLIGENCE SUMMARY.
(Erase heading not required.)

Instructions regarding War Diaries and Intelligence Summaries are contained in F. S. Regs., Part II. and the Staff Manual respectively. Title pages will be prepared in manuscript.

2/2nd W. R. Field Ambulance

Place	Date	Hour	Summary of Events and Information	Remarks and references to Appendices
BETHENCOURT	23.XII.17		Nothing to Report	—
BETHENCOURT	24.XII.17		do	—
BETHENCOURT	25.XII.17		do	—
BETHENCOURT	26.XII.17		do	—
BETHENCOURT	27.XII.17		CAPT. G. STEILL R.A.M.C. (T.C.) reported to this unit for duty and was taken on the strength accordingly	—
BETHENCOURT	28.XII.17		Nothing to Report	—
BETHENCOURT	29.XII.17		The Divisional GAS officer visited this unit & tested the men in their Gas Helmet drill & inspected their S.B. Respirator	—
BETHENCOURT	30.XII.17		Nothing to Report	—
BETHENCOURT	31.XII.17		do	—

Lieut. Colonel, R.A.M.C. (T.)
Commanding 2/2nd W.R. Field Ambulance

'MEDICAL'

ORIGINAL

Ja 13

140/2696

Confidential

2/2nd W. R. Field Ambulance.

War Diary

from 1st Jany. 1918 to 31 Jany 1918

Volume 13.

COMMITTEE FOR THE
MEDICAL HISTORY OF THE WAR
Date 4 MAR. 1918

Original "MEDICAL"

Army Form C.

WAR DIARY
or
INTELLIGENCE SUMMARY.
(Erase heading not required.)

2/2nd W. R. Field Ambulance. Sheet 1

Instructions regarding War Diaries and Intelligence Summaries are contained in F. S. Regs., Part II. and the Staff Manual respectively. Title pages will be prepared in manuscript.

Place	Date	Hour	Summary of Events and Information	Remarks and references to Appendices
BETHENCOURT	1.1.18		The unit is still in billets at BETHIAN COURT, drawing with local Supr a 188th Inf Bde.	Local Sch.
BETHENCOURT	2.1.18		158181 O.G. CUNNINGHAM having reported to arrival reinforcement on the 1.1.18	Sch.
BETHENCOURT	3.1.18		Lt Col EAMES G.W. proceeded to England on 14 days leave. CAPT. LANG, E.O. in command during his absence.	CAPT Lo
BETHENCOURT	4.1.18		603514 Pte HUMBY S. admitted to XIII Corps Rest Station 28/12/17 (Sick) T. LIEUT HUTCHINSON, R.C. returned from temp duty with 76 A.g.W. Fld Sch.	
BETHENCOURT	5.1.18		Unit received for inclusion by G.O.C. 62nd Div. two recommended reports to HQ.D.S.H.M. (403387 Cpl MILLERY J. & 403249 Pte ACKERMAN G.) (recommended military medal)	Sch.
			403/284 Cpl. WARWICK H. had admitted to XIII Corps Rest Station (Sick) on 2.1.18	
			19691 Pte POWICK M. (P.B.) was attacked) admitted to XIII Corps C.R.S. (Sick) on 1.1.18	Sch.

Original

Army Form C. 2118

WAR DIARY
or
INTELLIGENCE SUMMARY.
(Erase heading not required.)

2/2nd W.R. Field Ambulance. Sheet 2

Place	Date	Hour	Summary of Events and Information	Remarks and references to Appendices
BETHENCOURT	6.1.18		40514 Pte MUMBY, S. discharged to duty from XIII C.R.S. on 6.1.18	
			11699 Pte SAVOURY F (PB man attached) reported to O.C. XIII Corps Reinforcement Camp at TROISGHEM. Lost two packs of tooth duty, 9 pr of linen in billets, destroying suit of big slips & some greatcoats & one flashing than HQ 62nd Div notified pr	
BETHENCOURT	7.1.18		40330 Spr PENNY, T returned from 14 days leave to England. 40334 H/Cp. ROBERTS, T. admitted to 2/2 W.R.F.A. & transferred to 30 CCS Same day	2/2 W.R.F.A. & Kinchard & 42 CCS (sick) Pr
BETHENCOURT	8.1.18		43590 Pte TRURAN admitted by cases from BETHENCOURT to MAROGULE. He was moved by Ambulance 17.30 hrs arriving 9 A.M. & knowing 12.30 hrs. Examined books over a Hospital for Slight Gas Cases Mem 93rd Field Ambulance. Men returned S.I.O. L4 & 29 Capt. W.A COATS. R.A.M.O (TC) admitted be advised to 9.1.18 return to his Strength accordingly Capt. B RENHAM ST RAMO (TC) having reported his arrival as no/c 2/6 KOYLI on 3/1/18 is struck off the Strength from that date Pr	

T2134. Wt. W708—776. 50C000. 4/15. Sir J. C. & S.

Original

Army Form C. 2118

Instructions regarding War Diaries and Intelligence Summaries are contained in F. S. Regs., Part II. and the Staff Manual respectively. Title pages will be prepared in manuscript.

WAR DIARY
or
INTELLIGENCE SUMMARY.
(Erase heading not required.)

2/2nd W. R. Field Ambulance. Sheet 3

Place	Date	Hour	Summary of Events and Information	Remarks and references to Appendices
MAROEUIL	9.1.18		Pte Dainler notes cond. reported to 2/3 WR Fld Amb. Working party of 3 NCOs + 38 men to WR under Town Major. CAPT. ANDERSON, A. RAMC,T. + 403551 9.St. PARKER,T. 1st Army School of Instruction at BRUAY (22 days) Pk.	
MAROEUIL	10.1.18		W.Y.Q.M. NEWBOULT F.W. proceeded on 14 days leave to England. 403041 Pk GABBOTT H. proceeded to XIII Corps School of Sanitation Rt. on 10.1.18. In 7 days Course of instruction	
MAROEUIL	11.1.18		403529 Pk ASTCLIFFE, S. returned from 14 days leave to England 403560 Pk CHADWICK, S. proceeded on 14 days leave to England on 5/1/18. 47843 Pk ASHTON, C. proceeded on 14 days leave to England on 4/1/18 Pk. 403184 CM. HARDWICK, H. returned to duty from XIII Cor S. on 11/1/18. 45200 A. WISDOM, R. proceeded on 14 days leave to England on 9/1/18 CAPT. HALLIGAN, AMC RAMC TR. proceeded to XIII CorS. In temporary duty.	
MAROEUIL	12.1.18		2 NCOs + 30 men proceeds to 2/3 W R Fld Amb for fatigue duty in forward area.	

Original

Army Form C.2118

WAR DIARY
or
INTELLIGENCE SUMMARY
(Erase heading not required.)

2/2nd W.R. Field Ambulance. Sheet 4

Instructions regarding War Diaries and Intelligence Summaries are contained in F.S. Regs, Part II. and the Staff Manual respectively. Title pages will be prepared in manuscript.

Place	Date	Hour	Summary of Events and Information	Remarks and references to Appendices
MARŒUIL	12/1/18		40380 A/Cpl RHODES, E. admitted to 21 C.C.S. (sick) on 2/1/17 struck off his strength from that date	Ph.
MARŒUIL	13/1/18		M2/188071 Pte. SWANSON, A. ('M.T. A.S.C. attached) proceeded to England on 14 days leave	Ph.
MARŒUIL	14/1/18		403241 Cpl. ANDERSON, A. & A/Sgt. Parker, T. proceeded to 1st Army School of Instruction	
			403241 Pte. GABBOTT, J. proceeded to 13th Corps School of Sanitation 15/1/18	
			Capt. HALLIGAN, A.M.S. attached to 15th C.C.S. was evacuated to 42 C.C.S. (sick) on 13.1.18	
			1 M.C.O. & 11 men proceeded to 2/3rd W.R.F.A. in temporary duty.	
			43383 Sgt. NAMAR, A. returned from 14 days leave in England on 4.1.18.	
			T4/253770 Sgt. TATE, J. (577 Coy A.S.C. attached) proceeded to 12th Veterinary [Hosp?] on 4.12.17 & returned on 30.12.17	Ph.
MARŒUIL	15/1/18		nothing to report	
MARŒUIL	16/1/18		55042 L/c. ELLISTON, P. proceeded to 2/3 W.R.F.A. for temp duty	
			40478 Pte. BUTLER, J. returned from temp. duty with 2/3 W.R.F.A.	Ph.
MARŒUIL	17/1/18		19677 Pte. POWELL, T. transferred from 13th C.R.S. to 42 C.C.S. on 13/1/18 & is struck off his strength from that date	Ph.

Original

Army Form C. 2118

WAR DIARY
or
INTELLIGENCE SUMMARY.
(Erase heading not required.)

2/2nd W.R. Field Ambulance Sheet 1

Place	Date	Hour	Summary of Events and Information	Remarks and references to Appendices
MARŒUIL	18.1.18		14/241223 C.S.M. THOMSON J. attended ISSM with tour from 3.11.17	17.1.18
			463648. Pte PRINCE J. returned from 14 days leave on 17.1.18	
			46428 " BUTLER J. proceeded on " " on 18.1.18	
			34104 " PARKER B " " on 18-1-18	
			M²/050550 Pte HIGGINBOTHAM F (MT ASC) wd. in 14 days leave in France was admitted to 2nd Western General Hospital on 5.1.18 (S.C.R)	
			Lt Col. EAMES C.W. returned from 14 days leave in England Pk.	
MARŒUIL	19.1.18		CAPT. ANDERSON A and S/Sgt PARKER T. returned from 1st Army School of Instruction	DI
MARŒUIL	20.1.18		43784 Pte PATERSON J. proceeded on 14 days leave to England Pt.	
			403344 01H/Sgt ROBERTS T. attached as reinforcement in dischange from 4/2 aa8 has taken in the strength from 20.1.18 Pt.	
MARŒUIL	21.1.18		403530 Pte SUDDARDS W returned from tour duty with 2/5 WRFA on 16.1.18	17.1.18
			M²/102961 Pte HARRIS H " " " "	"
			M²/183099 Pte SMITH A proceeded " " " "	17.1.18

Original

Army Form C. 2118

WAR DIARY
or
INTELLIGENCE SUMMARY.
(Erase heading not required.)

2/2nd W. R. Field Ambulance. Sheet b

Instructions regarding War Diaries and Intelligence
Summaries are contained in F. S. Regs., Part II.
and the Staff Manual respectively. Title pages
will be prepared in manuscript.

Place	Date	Hour	Summary of Events and Information	Remarks and references to Appendices
MARŒUIL	21.1.18		MS/5537 Pte WHEELER, A. proceeded to temp duty to 2/3 WRFA on 19.1.18	Pte
MARŒUIL	22.1.18		403223 QMS WRIGHT, E. proceeded on 14 days leave to England on 22.1.18.	
			41843 Pte ASHTON, C.E returned from 14 days leave to England on 21.1.18 absent with out leave from 9.30 pm 21.1.18 to 9.30 pm 21.1.18	
			Awarded 3 days F.P. no 2, forfeits 2 days pay under R.W. and 1 G.O Bdy	
			1 NCO & 11 men proceeded for temp. duty to 2/3 WR FA on 22.1.18	
			14629 Pte JACKSON, F. whilst on temp. duty with 2/3 WR Fd Amb was admitted to 13th CCS (Sick) on 19.1.18	Pte
MARŒUIL	23.1.18		403560 Pte CHADWICK SB. returned from 14 days leave in England on 23.1.18	Pte
MARŒUIL	24.1.18		S/OT. ANDERSON A proceeded for temp. duty with 78 W Yorks Regt on 24.1.18	
			403342 Pte WHITELEY, W. proceeded on 14 days leave to England on 24.1.18	
MARŒUIL	25.1.18		403125 Pte GLADSTONE F. and 403478 Pte ROMAN, G. were awarded 7 days C.B. for an offence committed whilst on 23.1.18	
			403040 6/104 GRAY O.W. proceeded to 13th Corps School of Sanitation on 24.1.18	

Original

Army Form C. 2118.

WAR DIARY
or
INTELLIGENCE SUMMARY.
(Erase heading not required.)

2/2nd W.R. Field Ambulance. Army

Instructions regarding War Diaries and Intelligence Summaries are contained in F.S. Regs., Part II. and the Staff Manual respectively. Title pages will be prepared in manuscript.

Place	Date	Hour	Summary of Events and Information	Remarks and references to Appendices
MARŒUIL	25/1/18		M2/188099 Pte SMITH, A. and MS/5337 Pte WHEELER, A. returned from hosp. duty with 2/3 WR Fd Amb. on 26.1.18. Rd Dy.	
MARŒUIL	26/1/18		Nothing to report.	
MARŒUIL	26/1/18		74629 Pte JACKSON F ditch is duty from 13 CCRS on 26.1.18. Rd.	
MARŒUIL	27/1/18		6 O.R. joined for temp. duty with 2/3 WR F.A. on 27.1.18.	
			CAPT. HALLIGAN. A.M.T discharged to duty (temp duty) at (3 CRS) from 42 CCS on 27.1.18.	
			403164 Cpl. Hardwick H. proceeded on 14 days leave on 26.1.18 UK	
MARŒUIL	28/1/18		Hon LIEUT Y qm NEWBOULT FW returned from 14 days leave on 27/1/18 Rd.	
			403521 Pte WRIGHT F was admitted to 13 CRS (Sick) Rd	
MARŒUIL	28/1/18		on 28/1/18 jurnings. q Staves were reported by RE & leave extended.	
			45260 Pte WISDOM R returned from 14 days leave in England on the 28.1.18. 7M/253771 Sgt TOLLERTON J. proceeded on 14 days leave to England on 29.1.18	
			31814 Pte ISON H (PB attached) and 403523 Pte GRAY J with 1 motor car + 2 medics returned from temp duty with Camp Commandant, 62 nd Divn W.	

Original

Army Form C. 2118.

WAR DIARY
or
INTELLIGENCE SUMMARY.
(Erase heading not required.)

2/2nd W.R. Field Ambulance. Sheet 6

Instructions regarding War Diaries and Intelligence Summaries are contained in F. S. Regs., Part II. and the Staff Manual respectively. Title pages will be prepared in manuscript.

Place	Date	Hour	Summary of Events and Information	Remarks and references to Appendices
MAROEUIL	29.1.18		TEMP. CAPT COATS. W.A. proceeded to England on 29.1.18 on completion of contract and is struck off strength accordingly.	DL
MAROEUIL	30.1.18		3 arrivals and 3 pairs of H.D. horses returned to Town Major on 30.1.18 to assist in farm work. 403648 Pte PRINGE J. was admitted to 5/2 WR Fld Amb (Sick) on 28.1.18 and transferred to 59 C.C.S. on 30.1.18 & was struck off for Strength accordingly. 1 NCO & 4 men (matic duty) proceeded from 7/5 Dgn Rgt) arrived on duty on 30.1.18. An later on the Strength accordingly. Pte DEWHURST 4 proceeded to England on 14 days leave on 19.1.18.	DL
MAROEUIL	31.1.18		403268 Pte JACKSON E. W.R. on temp. duty at 13 CCS was admitted to 42 CCS on 28.1.18 & is Struck off the Strength accordingly. 403323 Pte MASSEY A. returned from temp. duty at 13th CCS on 31.1.18	

Original

Army Form C. 2118.

Instructions regarding War Diaries and Intelligence Summaries are contained in F.S. Regs., Part II. and the Staff Manual respectively. Title pages will be prepared in manuscript.

WAR DIARY
or
INTELLIGENCE SUMMARY.
(Erase heading not required.)

Army Form C. 2118.

2/2nd W.R. Field Ambulance. Sheet 9

Place	Date	Hour	Summary of Events and Information	Remarks and references to Appendices
MARŒUIL	31·1·18		403650 Pte McWILLIAMS E returned from temp duty with 2/3 W.R Fd Amb. on 30/1/18	
			403218 Pte WADE G proceeded to 2/3 WR Fd Amb. for temp duty on 30·1·18 vice Pte McWILLIAMS.	
			403793 Pte FIELDHOUSE G and 403209 Pte RICHARDS W proceeded to 13th CCS for hosp. duty on 31·1·18 vice Pte MASSEY and Pte JACKSON.	
			1 NCO + 2 men (walk duty personnel from 76 Dn Rgt) returned thro' arrival on 31·1·18 + are taken on the strength.	
			The W/m NCO + men proceeding on 14 days leave to England on 31/1/18	
			M/188571 Cpl GILLESPIE T (ASC att) T/368134 Pte CUNNINGHAM G 403515 Pte WHALLEY M and 403323 Pte MASSEY A. M²/050590 Pte HEGINBOTHAM F. is Struck off the Strength from 3/1/18	
			403521 Pte WRIGHT A and transfers from 13th CCS to 42 CCS on 29·1·18 + is Struck on his Strength accordingly.	S.O.

E M Rainey
Lieut. Colonel. R.A.M.C.(T)
Chang. Capt. Rainy
Comdg. 2/2nd W.R. F.A.
In O/C 2/2nd W.R. Field Ambulance.

140/2784

2/3rd West Riding F.A.

COMMITTEE FOR THE
MEDICAL HISTORY OF THE WAR
Date -8 APR 1918

MEDICAL

Confidential

War Diary

of

2/2 West Riding Field Ambce

from Feby 1/1918 to Feby 28/1918

Volume 14

MEDICAL

Army Form C. 2118.

WAR DIARY
or
INTELLIGENCE SUMMARY.
(Erase heading not required.)

Instructions regarding War Diaries and Intelligence Summaries are contained in F. S. Regs., Part II. and the Staff Manual respectively. Title pages will be prepared in manuscript.

Place	Date	Hour	Summary of Events and Information	Remarks and references to Appendices
MARGUIL	1.2.18		We unit is still running Dressing Station in Gezard Causs and also attaining slight cases for 3 days, evacuation to C.R.S.	
			Lieut. SHERRICK J.W. Mo.R.O. U.S.A. attached for study, has 2/5 D&W Regt. to return in strength from 1.2.18	
			T. Capt. WILSON F.R. RAMC attached for study from 7/6 D&W Regt. to return on the strength from 1.2.18 Lgt. Rec.	
MARGUIL	2.2.18		nothing to report.	Rec.
MARGUIL	3.2.18		do.	Rec.
MARGUIL	4.2.18		T. Capt. BRENNAN S.J. RAMC attached for study from 2/5 KOYLI to return on his strength from 4.2.18 Rec.	
MARGUIL	5.2.18		nothing to report.	Rec.
MARGUIL	6.2.18		T. Capt. BRENNAN S.J. RAMC transferred to duty to 5th K.O.Y.L.I. to struck of his strength from 6.2.18 Rec.	
MARGUIL	7.2.18		nothing to report.	Rec.
MARGUIL	8.2.18		53 O.R. returned from trench duty with 2/5 W.R. Regt. Curb. Rec.	

Army Form C. 2118.

WAR DIARY
or
INTELLIGENCE SUMMARY.
(Erase heading not required.)

Instructions regarding War Diaries and Intelligence Summaries are contained in F. S. Regs., Part II. and the Staff Manual respectively. Title pages will be prepared in manuscript.

Place	Date	Hour	Summary of Events and Information	Remarks and references to Appendices
MARGUIL	9.2.18		Arena duty from 2/3 London Fd. and. and arrived to car and Dressing Station. Plan of Site is attached.	Pl.
MARGUIL	10.2.18		The unit having handed over to 2/3 London Fd. Amb. 56th Div. marched by road to BAILLEUL AUX CORNAILLES and was accommodated in billets	
			that informer Sunt. 36.B. U.19.a.9.4. The unit is dealing with Sick from 186 Inf. Bde., the Sick being returned to their held ambulance Pl.	
BAILLEUL AUX CORNAILLES	11.2.18		LIEUT. SHERRICK J.W. M.O.R.C. USA is struck off the strength from 7.2.18 having been posted for duty to 5th or 9 W Rgt Pl.	
BAILLEUL	12.2.18		LT-COL. EAMES G.W. R.A.M.C. T. proceed to H.Q. 62nd Div. on temp. duty as ADMS.	Pl.
BAILLEUL	13.2.18		29 O.R. from 11.2.18 reported as min knowank, and taken on strength, having whilst in rest, completing the following Physical training, Squad drill and Stretcher will.	

Army Form C. 2118.

WAR DIARY
or
INTELLIGENCE SUMMARY.
(Erase heading not required.)

Place	Date	Hour	Summary of Events and Information	Remarks and references to Appendices
BAILLEUL AUX CORNAILLES	13/2/18		Drill in S.B.R. Saluting drill, Stretcher bearing drill. The drill. Route marches. Company drill. Carrying wounded in trenches. mat making. Training in use of gromet extricated over drill. Lectures on also hang guns. in the following, Recruitment & treatment of Sick, arrest of hounding, Application of trench splint. Duties of N.C.Os. Discipline. Savory "heated Sanitation and the influence of his kit in the prevention of skin disease	Pte
BAILLEUL	14/2/18		hatching to return	Pte
BAILLEUL	15/2/18		having to return	At
BAILLEUL	16/2/18		11 O.R. NEW ARMIES & Regulars transferred to return to duty to A.D.M.S. 31st Div. 16 OR T.F. transferred to return to duty to ADMS 56th Div	Pte Ot
BAILLEUL	17/2/18		7 OR his army returns as underneath. nim 17.2.18 on the strength	Pte Ot

Army Form C. 2118.

WAR DIARY
or
INTELLIGENCE SUMMARY.
(Erase heading not required.)

Place	Date	Hour	Summary of Events and Information	Remarks and references to Appendices
BAILLEUL	18.2.18		CAPT. KENWORTHY T.R. M.C. RAMC. returned to duty & is taken on the Strength from 18.2.18	R.
BAILLEUL	19.2.18		Nothing to report	R.
BAILLEUL	20.2.18		1 O.R. has Army attached as Reinforcement & is taken on Strength from 20.2.18	R.
BAILLEUL	21.2.18		Nothing to report.	R.
BAILLEUL	22.2.18		8 O.R. has Army proceeded to report to BOnS 31st Div R.l.	R.
BAILLEUL	23.2.18		nothing to report	R.
BAILLEUL	24.2.18		nothing to report.	R. S.A.
BAILLEUL	25.2.18		nothing to report	R.
BAILLEUL	26.2.18		nothing to report.	R.
BAILLEUL	27.2.18		T/Capt STIELL G. and 29 O.R. proceeded to ROCLINCOURT take over A.D.S. at TUNNEL DUMP from 94th Fd. Amb. 31st Div on Feb. 28th. Map reference Sheet 51 B. B15 C.S.4.	R.
BAILLEUL	28.2.18		T/Capt WILSON F.R. and 26 O.R. proceeded to ROCLINCOURT to take over A.D.S. at VANCOUVER ROAD on March 1st	R.

Army Form C. 2118.

WAR DIARY
or
INTELLIGENCE SUMMARY.
(Erase heading not required.)

Instructions regarding War Diaries and Intelligence Summaries are contained in F. S. Regs., Part II. and the Staff Manual respectively. Title pages will be prepared in manuscript.

Place	Date	Hour	Summary of Events and Information	Remarks and references to Appendices
BAILLEUL	Feb 18		Form 9th Field of Ambulance : trop shewn Out 17 18 Dr. B 3 16 9 3 Strong ask Roundchums 6 W. Raws 60 7/2 N. R. Fed amb.	

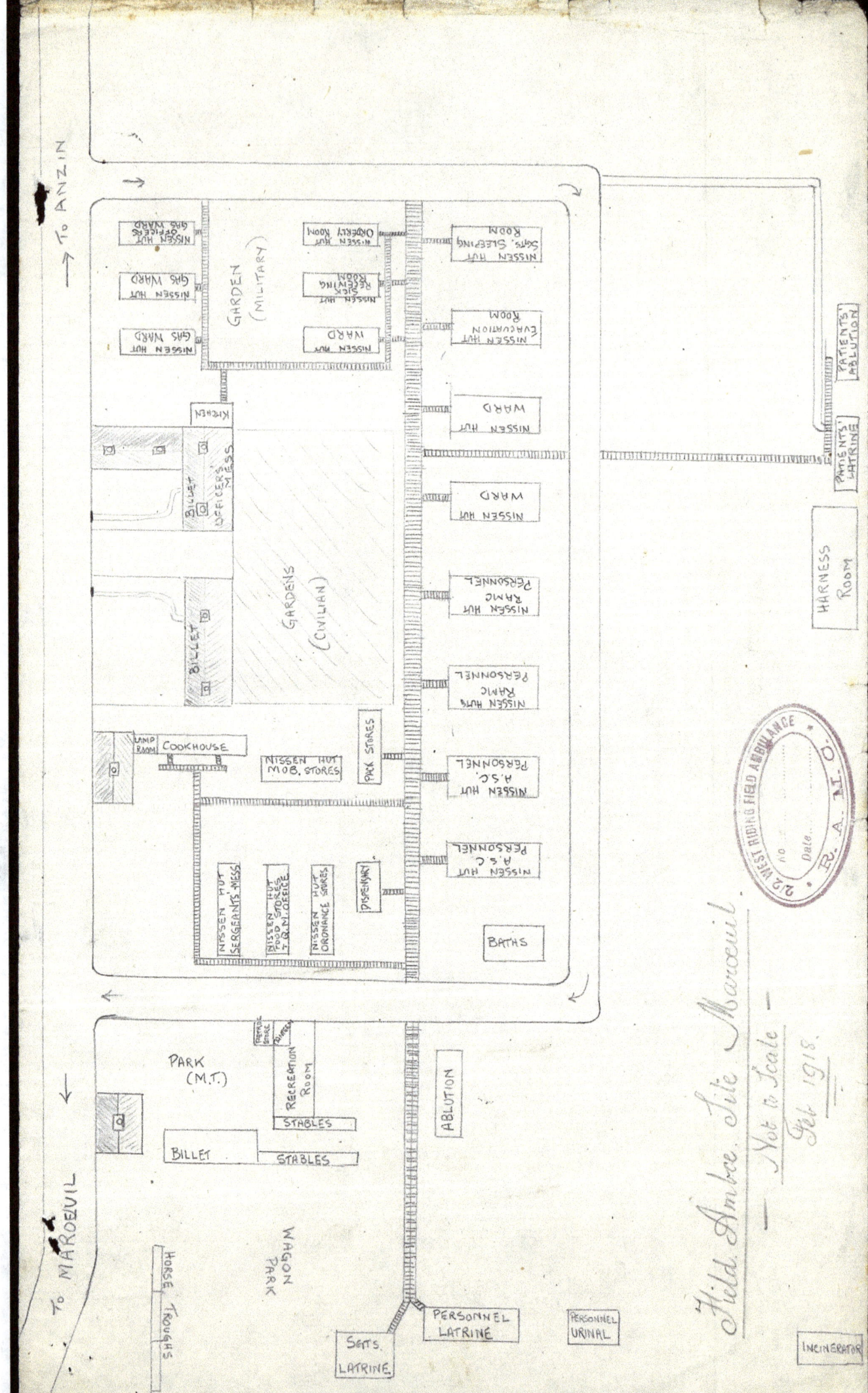

2/2nd West Riding F.A.

COMMITTEE FOR THE
MEDICAL HISTORY OF THE WAR
Date 12 MAY 1918

MEDICAL Sheet 1

Army Form C.

Vol 15

WAR DIARY
or
INTELLIGENCE SUMMARY.
(Erase heading not required.)

2/2nd W. R. Field Ambulance.

Instructions regarding War Diaries and Intelligence Summaries are contained in F.S. Regs., Part II. and the Staff Manual respectively. Title pages will be prepared in manuscript.

ORIGINAL

Place	Date	Hour	Summary of Events and Information	Remarks and references to Appendices
BAILLEUL AUX CORNAILLES	1.3.18		The unit is still in rest billets with the exception of his twelve such as 1 officer & 26 O.R. who have been attached to serve the advanced dressing stations from 4th In Field Amb. 30th Div. Pt.	
BAILLEUL	2.3.18		CAPT. KANG, E.C. & 12 O.R. proceeded to ROBINCOURT L.R. and main D dressing station from 4th Field amb Pt.	
BAILLEUL	3.3.18		The remainder of the unit under LIEUT-COL. EAMES D.M. proceeded to ROBINCOURT to man Dressing Station Rear Road transport by train from TINQUES, transport by road Pt.	
ROBINCOURT	4.3.18		hitherto & posts of evacuation from forward area. Regt Sotr, in TOMMY ALLEY at B.12 & 4.5. (Street 51 B) personnel. 4 men R and attached. 1st Relay Post in Tommy alley at B11 d 88. personnel 4 men R and. 2nd Relay Post. in Tommy alley at B.16. 6 44. Personnel 1 NCO & 4 men. A.D.S. at TUNNEL DUMP in Sunken road at B.15. c.5.1.	

Sheet 2

Army Form C.

WAR DIARY
or
INTELLIGENCE SUMMARY.
(Erase heading not required.)

Instructions regarding War Diaries and Intelligence Summaries are contained in F. S. Regs., Part II. and the Staff Manual respectively. Title pages will be prepared in manuscript.

212nd W. R. Field Ambulance.

Place	Date	Hour	Summary of Events and Information	Remarks and references to Appendices
Ecoivres	1.3.18		Personnel 1 officer 1 NCO (S.Sgt) 16 men accommodation in 10 stretcher cases and 30 sitting cases of moment. There is a clothing store for reclothing gassed cases, also a bath house & Sout Kitchen run by the Division. Methods of evacuation. By day. Hand carry along OUSE ALLEY to DAYLIGHT RAILHEAD at B.19 central. In dull weather a hand trolley can be used as far as Daylight Railroad from Tunnel Dump. Allandale Route. Hand carry along MOR WALK & Sch. of entrenchment to ARRAS - BAILLEUL Road and along road to MAISON DE LA COTE, thence by car to MDS. N.B. This road is outside the Divisional area. By night. Light Railway from Tunnel Dump to M.D.S. (there is a siding in the M.D.S.) This is a special ambulance truck accommodating 8 stretcher cases	

Sheet 3

Army Form C.

WAR DIARY
or
INTELLIGENCE SUMMARY.
(Erase heading not required.)

2/2nd W. R. Field Ambulance.

Place	Date	Hour	Summary of Events and Information	Remarks and references to Appendices
ROCLINCOURT	4.3.18		Further tracks can be obtained by applying to Divisional Hqrs Railway Officer at Roclincourt for Rain Gus at rations wing high & kings hook SOR y wounded from ADS. Lt Soln. R.A.P. is situated in HUDSON TRENCH at T.29 C.5.8. Personnel 4 men Round attached. 1st Relay Post at T.28 C.5.7. in HUDSON TRENCH Personnel 1 N.C.O. & 4 men Round. There is a double stretcher back down in trench from here to VANCOUVER ROAD and a wheeled stretcher can be used. Advanced Dressing Station is in VANCOUVER ROAD at B.3.C.9.4. Personnel 1 Officer, 1 Sgt. & 12 men. The accommodation for patients is good. Evacuation. By day, wheeled stretcher from A.D.S. to COMMANDANTS HOUSE and thence by car to M.D.S. By night, Car from A.D.S. to M.D.S.	

Sheet 4

Army Form C.

WAR DIARY
or
INTELLIGENCE SUMMARY.
(Erase heading not required.)

2/2nd W. R. Field Ambulance.

Place	Date	Hour	Summary of Events and Information	Remarks and references to Appendices
ROCLINCOURT	6.5.17		There is a light Railway from the A.D.S. running through WILLERVAL to M.D.S. but this is said to be unreliable. The Car comes up to the A.D.S. every morning after dusk & wounded S.C.R. & transported and again before daylight. y WILLERVAL is being shelled this is a case currently held from the A.D.S. to the R.R. crossing on WILLERVAL - FARBUS Road. Train Dressing Station at Roclincourt. Accommodation four bivvan huts our equipment as wards one for clerics one for wounded cases one for medical cases & one for Surgical S.O.P. cases. There are bivvans with tre Bapteme names Dressing & operating room Q.M. Stores & laundry Room are in Nissen huts. There are 7 hospital marquees in the rocklincourt on the adbrivation road, one in gas cases on for marquie cases, and three spare.	

Sheet 5

Army Form C.

WAR DIARY
or
INTELLIGENCE SUMMARY.
(Erase heading not required.)

212nd W. R. Field Amble 31/26

Place	Date	Hour	Summary of Events and Information	Remarks and references to Appendices
ROCLINCOURT	4.5.18		There is a small dental hut, where the dental Surgeon from 30 C.C.S. sees dental cases on Mondays, Tuesdays & Wednesdays. There are the usual administrative offices in small huts. In the rear of hostel stabling there are 3 elephant dug-outs. In latrines on the east side of the Camp. The personnel is accommodated in dug outs on the west side of the Camp. The transport lines are situated on the west side of the Camp. There are Good Standings for the animals much lines & harness room, and hire supply is working through. The ASC. MT personnel are accommodated in small shacks near the horse lines. The ASC MT are accommodated in small huts in ruined buildings. The MAC Cars are always parked at the MDS & extra Cars to hand in an attachment to ADMS. Evacuation is by car to 30 & 54 CCS. in alternate	

T.J134. Wt. W708-776. 500000. 4/15. Sir J. C. & S.

Sheet 6

Army Form C.

WAR DIARY
or
INTELLIGENCE SUMMARY.
(Erase heading not required.)

2/2nd W.R. Field Ambulance.

Place	Date	Hour	Summary of Events and Information	Remarks and references to Appendices
ROCLINCOURT	9.3.18		keep, and to 13th C.R.S. An alternative A.D.S. has been prepared by S¹ S¹ B.M in the right section at ORCHARD DUGOUT on the ARLEUX - SUGAR FACTORY Road at B.15.d.4.4. She moved Stretcher bearing parties from the front line considerably by carrying along Tommy delay and machine gun trench to a point opposite the ARLEUX - SUGAR factory road where a machine gun trench exists. She wound where a carry across the open to the Sun Run road of about 150 yards could then be worked. Stretcher down the road to the halfway A.D.S. Cars can come as far up as Orchard Dugout by the following road ARRAS - LENS Road - THELUS - COMMANDANT'S HOUSE, LONG WOOD, CRUCIFIX CORNER, SUCERIE to A.D.S. She present A.D.S. however is in front of RED LINE and in the event of the front line being captured	

Sheet 7.

Army Form C.

WAR DIARY
or
INTELLIGENCE SUMMARY.
(Erase heading not required.)

2/2nd W.R. Field Ambulance.

Place	Date	Hour	Summary of Events and Information	Remarks and references to Appendices
ROCLINCOURT	16.3.18		It would be impossible to evacuate patients. The dug-out is a deep one, with 3 entrances which are very steep, and would be difficult to get stretchers down, and the passages are very narrow in stretchers. A heating party of 2 men is carrying it from TUNNEL DUMP at present. Evacuation from forward area is A.D.S. at TUNNEL DUMP is difficult and also hare to be carried our the top in daylight. Evacuation would be much must easier if TOMMY ALLEY was cleaned out in presence returned to use. OUSE ALLEY which is in his next Divisional area this is a hour's road from ROCLINCOURT to near ARMY ADJANTS HOUSE which shortens the car journey from the left sector by about an kilometre, but it is is a but road for cars. Dr.	

T.J.134. Wt. W708-776. 50C000. 4/15. Sir J.C.&S.

Sheet 5

Army Form C. 2118.

WAR DIARY
or
INTELLIGENCE SUMMARY.
(Erase heading not required.)

2/2nd W.R. Field Ambulance

Place	Date	Hour	Summary of Events and Information	Remarks and references to Appendices
Roclincourt	5.3.18		Nothing to report.	Ok
Roclincourt	6.3.18		The A.D.S. at TUNNEL DUMP was heavily shelled this morning with 5.9 shells, and a direct hit on the H.Q. of the dug out for Ronnie personnel destroyed one dug out. Slightly injuring one man.	Ok
Roclincourt	7.3.18		Reconstruction of dug out commenced under supervision of R.E.	Ok
Roclincourt	8.3.18		Arrangements have been made by D.D.M.S. 13th Corps to obtain the use of the Heavy Artillery dug out at A.15.a.2.6. to use as an A.D.S. in the event of an enemy attack. Two dug outs in attack behind the Railway Embankment opened. Ho just dug out and one entered to be made dressing rooms. A stable tent was fitted up as an A.D.S. May possibly accommodate about 50 lying cases and a sign board from here being erected to Coy. and outside hands. & case carpet up to this A.D.S.	

Sheet 9

Army Form C. 2118.

WAR DIARY
or
INTELLIGENCE SUMMARY.
(Erase heading not required.)

2/2nd W.R. Field Ambulance

Place	Date	Hour	Summary of Events and Information	Remarks and references to Appendices
ROCLINCOURT	8.3.18		Sid dug out is about 400 yards from his Head near TIRED ALLEY made his entrenchments.	Plr D.C.
ROCLINCOURT	9.3.18		Nothing to report.	
ROCLINCOURT	10.3.18		4 men Round attached to Support R.A.P in VANCOUVER ROAD at B29 a 5.1. and 4 men Round to in Support R.A.P in CLYDE ALLEY at B10 C 2.8. Personnel at each A.D.S increased to provide to bearer Squads 8 stretchers to those returning to running to A.D.S. Pr returning to report	
ROCLINCOURT	11.3.18			
ROCLINCOURT	12.3.18		12 men from 2/3 W.R. Field Ambulance reported this morning to commence making & alleviating Post, and R.A.P. to Heavy Artillery near Plank Road at B29 b 2.4. During the afternoon information was received that an enemy offensive was anticipated next day, hurriedly sent down arrangements made to deal with the situation and personnel detailed to man duties. DL	

Sheet 10
Army Form C. 2118.

WAR DIARY
or
INTELLIGENCE SUMMARY.
(Erase heading not required.)

2/2nd W.R. Field Ambulance

Place	Date	Hour	Summary of Events and Information	Remarks and references to Appendices
ROCLINCOURT	13.3.18		The neighbourhood of ROCLINCOURT was shelled during the night by an enemy H.V. gun. No casualties.	R.b.
ROCLINCOURT	14.3.18		The main dressing station was again shelled during the course of the night, but no casualties occurred.	R.b.
ROCLINCOURT	15.3.18		The main dressing station was again shelled during the night, but no casualties occurred.	R.b.
ROCLINCOURT	16.3.18		About 150 cases of gas poisoning were received and evacuated to C.C.S. in the course of the day. The principal symptoms in all cases being intense conjunctivitis, with nausea and vomiting, many of the patients complained the smell of the gas as to "onions". There were no cases presenting dangerous symptoms.	R.b.
ROCLINCOURT	17.3.18		About 200 cases of shell gas poisoning were admitted and evacuated to C.C.S. during the day. Arrangements have been made to deal with casualties expected to occur in a raid carried out by 147th Duke of Wellington's	

T2134. Wt. W708—776. 500000. 4/15. Sir J. C. & S.

Army Form C. 2118.

WAR DIARY
or
INTELLIGENCE SUMMARY.
(Erase heading not required.)

2/2nd W.R. Field Ambulance

Place	Date	Hour	Summary of Events and Information	Remarks and references to Appendices
ROCLINCOURT	17/3/18		Regt. on left O.C. of Divisional front at 11 hrs on 17.3.18. The medical officers of 5th and 9th D. of W. Regt. are to proceed to R.A.P. to deal with casualties. The medical officer of 4th D. of W. Regt. is to assist at the A.D.S. 8 men R.A.M.C. Sent up to A.D.S. as extra hands. 6 bearer cars to proceed to THELUS - COMMANDANTS HOUSE Road at 11.30 p.m. to evacuate from front area. 3 Daimler cars from 4/3 W.R. Fd. Amb. and 4 from M.A.C. returned to M.D.S. to evacuate casualties to A.D.S. all serious cases to be taken direct from A.D.S. to C.C.S. TEMP LIEUT BASSETT R.J. RAMC having returned has arrived on 17.3.18 is taken on the strength accordingly.	

Sheet 12

Army Form C. 2118.

WAR DIARY
or
INTELLIGENCE SUMMARY.
(Erase heading not required.)

2/2nd W. R. Field Ambulance

Place	Date	Hour	Summary of Events and Information	Remarks and references to Appendices
ROCLINCOURT	18.3.18		nothing to report	
ROCLINCOURT	19.3.18		nothing to report	
ROCLINCOURT	20.3.18		nothing to report	
ROCLINCOURT	21.3.18		Main dressing Station at ROCLINCOURT	
ROCLINCOURT	22.3.18		and advanced dressing Stations at TUNNEL DUMP and VANCOUVER ROAD were inspected by D.M.S. 1st Army & D.D.M.S. 13th Corps.	
ROCLINCOURT	22.3.18		A.D.S. at TUNNEL DUMP. handed over to 10th Canadian Fd Amb.	
ROCLINCOURT	23.3.18		A.D.S. at VANCOUVER ROAD handed over to 8th Canadian Field ambulance.	
			The unit moved by road to 10th Canadian Field ambulance.	
MONT. ST ELOI	24.3.18		Surplus Kit dumped at Billet no 29, along with that of units of 186 Inf. Bde. Proceeded by road to WARLUS and arrived at 19th Corps Rest Station.	
WARLUS	25.3.18		Received orders at 2 A.M. to join 186 Inf. Bde. who were marching through WARLUS and hurried to AYETTE marched on at 5 a.m. in rear of 186 Inf. Bde. and	

Sheet 13

Army Form C. 2118.

WAR DIARY
or
INTELLIGENCE SUMMARY.
(Erase heading not required.)

212nd W. R. Field Ambulance.

Place	Date	Hour	Summary of Events and Information	Remarks and references to Appendices
WARLUS	25.3.18		Halted on Side of road about half a mile South West of BUCQUOY. 2 Bearer Subdivisions under MAJOR LANG and CAPT WILSON Sent forward to establish advanced dressing Station between BUCQUOY and ACHIET LE PETIT in an old Field Ambulance Sdt. to awowate Casualties from the 185th Y 186th Inf. Bdes. who were holding a line in front of ACHIET LE PETIT. On not of the 186th homeward while halted Pl.	
BUCQUOY	26.3.18		About 5 am. information was received that the infantry had evacuated the line held the previous night and was taking up a post line about 400 yards East of BUCQUOY. A.D.S. party was withdrawn & Sdt. where it was bivouacked. A party 4 bearers under CAPT. HALLIGAN established an advanced post in a trench about 400 yards west of BUCQUOY on the Sonth of BUCQUOY- HANNESCAMPS road LIEUT. BASSETT with a heavy Subdivision opened an	

Sheet 14

Army Form C. 2118.

WAR DIARY
or
INTELLIGENCE SUMMARY.
(Erase heading not required.)

2/2nd W. R. Field Ambulance.

Place	Date	Hour	Summary of Events and Information	Remarks and references to Appendices
BUCQUOY	26/3/18		Advanced dressing Station at cross roads in HANNESCAMPS. Remainder of unit proceeded by road to HUMBERCAMPS and opened a main dressing Station in some farm buildings. Several hundred casualties were dealt with during the course of the day.	R.
HUMBERCAMPS	27/3/18		Main dressing Station handed over to 71st W.R. Fd. Amb.	R.
HUMBERCAMPS	28/3/18		The unit is now responsible solely for evacuation from left Station of forward area. Additional MO's and bearers sent up to reinforce A.D.S. Shelled and thus fore moved to west end of HANNESCAMP where there is a wooden hut used as dressing room, with two cellars and some shallow dug-outs. Relay posts established east and west of ESSARTS on BUCQUOY - HANNESCAMPS road. Evacuation by wheeled Stretcher to A.D.S. Y thence by horsed ambulance to M.D.S.	Ct.
HUMBERCAMPS	29/3/18		Car central post established in BIENVILLERS and horsed ambulance kept at hand in reserve. Open field ambulance is kept at A.D.S.	R.

Sheet 15

Army Form C. 2118.

WAR DIARY
or
INTELLIGENCE SUMMARY.
(Erase heading not required.)

2/2nd W.R. Field Ambulance

Place	Date	Hour	Summary of Events and Information	Remarks and references to Appendices
LUMBRES CAMPS	30.3.18		30 men of Divisional Band attached as additional bearers in case of necessity. Sir Madgwick to be not wounded by road to ST. LEGER L'AUTHIE	
ST. LEGER L'AUTHIE	3.3.18		Orders received to hand over positions in forward area to 48th Field Ambulance. 31st Div. Commence relieving during the morning, hour from forward area increasing to ST. LEGER Rd. as being relieved	

C. R. Burns
Lieut. Colonel. R.A.M.C.(T)
Commanding. 2/2nd W.R. Field Ambulance.

[Stamp: 2/2 WEST RIDING FIELD AMBULANCE R.A.M.O.]

140/2700

2/2 West Riding Field Ambulance

COMMITTEE FOR THE
MEDICAL HISTORY
Date -6 JUN 1918

April 1918

ORIGINAL

Confidential   Vol 16

War Diary
of

2/2nd W.R. Field Ambulance,

From 1st April 1918 to 30th April 1918

Volume 16

Army Form C. 2118.

WAR DIARY
or
INTELLIGENCE SUMMARY.
(Erase heading not required.)

2/2nd W.R. Field Ambulance

Sheet 1

ORIGINAL

Place	Date	Hour	Summary of Events and Information	Remarks and references to Appendices
ST LEGER	1.4.18		The unit is in rest billets, attached to 187 Inf. Bde., and moving with said S.R. who are operating to No 3 Canadian Stationary Hospital at BOULOGNE.	Rd.
ST LEGER	2.4.18		Having to return.	Rd.
ST LEGER	3.4.18		31 men of Divisional Band who had been attached for use as Stretcher bearers rejoined returned to their Bns.	Rd.
			that band parties having to return	Rd.
ST LEGER	4.4.18		nothing to report	Rd.
ST LEGER	5.4.18		nothing	Rd.
ST LEGER	6.4.18		Major ANDERSON A. and 12 O.R. proceeded to SOUASTRE as advance party to take over Main Dressing Station from 1/5th East. Lancs Fld. Amb. 42nd Divn Rd.	Rd.
ST LEGER	7.4.18		2 Squads of bearers attached to each battalion of 187th Inf. Bde. to work between R.A.P. and 1st Relay Post when in the line.	
			The remainder of the unit marched to SOUASTRE	

Army Form C. 2118.

WAR DIARY
or
INTELLIGENCE SUMMARY.
(Erase heading not required.)

2/2nd W.R. Field Ambulance

Sheet 2

Place	Date	Hour	Summary of Events and Information	Remarks and references to Appendices
St. LEGER	7.4.18		and K.O.R own M.D.S. from 1/5" East hours. Red Cross Lames put them in at	Rt.
SOUASTRE	8.4.18		HENU. From Divising Station is Situated in School buildings at cross roads. Accommodation for Stretcher cases with dressing room and dispensing	
			Officers accommodated in Cinema Hall at hear of School and for Gassed Cases in barns behind	
			Sick are being evacuated by 2/1 S" W.R. Field Amb Evacuation by W. 21 M.A.C. Cars to 3 Canadian Stationary Hospital, DOULLENS or to 6 Stationary Hospital, FREVENT.	Dr. Rt.
SOUASTRE	9.4.18		Loading is relied.	
SOUASTRE	10.4.18		2 NCOs and 32 men attached to 2/3 W.R. Fld. Amb. to assist in clearing forward area	Rt.

WAR DIARY
or
INTELLIGENCE SUMMARY

Army Form C. 2118.

2/2nd W.R. Field Ambulance

Sheet 3

Place	Date	Hour	Summary of Events and Information	Remarks and references to Appendices
SOUASTRE	11.4.18		CAPT. A.M.S. HALLIGAN. R.A.M.C. (T.C.) proceeded to the 313th Brigade R.F.A. to take over the duties of Medical Officer	
SOUASTRE	12.4.18		Nothing to Report	a.a.
SOUASTRE	13.4.18		Nothing to Report	a.a.
SOUASTRE	14.4.18		LIEUT R.J. BASSETT. R.A.M.C. (T.C.) 1 N.C.O. & 12 O/R proceeded to No. 3 Canadian Stationary Hospital for temporary duty	a.a.
SOUASTRE	15.4.18		1 N.C.O. & 16 O/R of the 2/7th W.R. Regt. 1 N.C.O. & 16 O/R from the 2/4 W.R. Regt. & 16 O/R from the 5th W.R. Regt. reported for duty to this unit to act as stretcher bearers in the forward area	a.a.
SOUASTRE	16.4.18		LIEUT. O. SINCUR. A.M.C. proceeded to the 5th W.R. Regt. as M.O. i/c vice CAPT. T.R. WILSON. R.A.M.C. (T.C.)	a.a.
SOUASTRE	17.4.18		Nothing to Report	a.a.
SOUASTRE	18.4.18		MAJOR E.C. LANG. D.S.O. R.A.M.C. proceeded to the 94th Field Ambulance to take over command of the unit	a.a.
SOUASTRE	19.4.18		Nothing to Report	a.a.
SOUASTRE	20.4.18		Nothing to Report	a.a.

Army Form C. 2118.

WAR DIARY
or
INTELLIGENCE SUMMARY.

(Erase heading not required.)

2/2nd W.R. Field Ambulance

Instructions regarding War Diaries and Intelligence Summaries are contained in F.S. Regs., Part II. and the Staff Manual respectively. Title pages will be prepared in manuscript.

Place	Date	Hour	Summary of Events and Information	Remarks and references to Appendices
SOUASTRE	21.4.18		LIEUT A WINFIELD R.A.M.C. (S.R) reported for duty	S.A.W-4
SOUASTRE	22.4.18		Nothing to report	aa
SOUASTRE	23.4.18		Nothing to report	aa
SOUASTRE	24.4.18		2 NCOs & 32 o/r attached to the 2/3 W R Field Amb returned to their unit	aa
			The M.D.S. SOUASTRE was handed over to the 48th Field Ambulance (37th Div)	aa
			The Unit proceeded by road to ST LEGER L'ARTHIE	aa
ST LEGER	25.5.18		The 50 men attached from the Battalion of the 186? Inf Brigade reported to the	aa
			62nd DIVISIONAL WING. The Unit is in rest billets	aa
ST LEGER	26.5.18		Nothing to report	aa
ST LEGER	27.5.18		Nothing to report	aa
ST LEGER	28.5.18		Nothing to report	aa
ST LEGER	29.5.18		Nothing to report	aa
ST LEGER	30.5.18		Nothing to report	aa

Lieut. Colonel, R.A.M.C.(T).
Commanding 2/2nd W.R. Field Ambulance.

(MEDICAL)

WD 17
140/2983

ORIGINAL Confidential

War Diary

of

2/2nd W.R. Field Ambulance.

from 1st May 1918 to 31st May 1918

Volume 17.

COMMITTEE FOR THE
MEDICAL HISTORY OF THE WAR
Date 9 JUL 1918

(MEDICAL)
Army Form C. 2118.

WAR DIARY
or
INTELLIGENCE SUMMARY.
(Erase heading not required.)

Instructions regarding War Diaries and Intelligence Summaries are contained in F.S. Regs., Part II. and the Staff Manual respectively. Title pages will be prepared in manuscript.

*[Stamp: 2/2nd WEST RIDING FIELD AMBULANCE * R.A.M.C. (T)]*

Place	Date	Hour	Summary of Events and Information	Remarks and references to Appendices
ST LEGER L'AUTHIE	1.V.18		Unit in rest billets. Evacuating Brigade Sick	aa
ST LEGER	2.V.18		CAPT. E.M. ASHCROFT RAMC (T.C) & LIEUT C.M. CRAWFORD reported for duty	aa
			CAPT. G.G. JACK RAMC (SR) reported for duty. LIEUT. BASSETT RAMC (TC) returned to this unit from duty with the 3rd CANADIAN ST HOSPITAL DOULLENS.	aa
ST LEGER	3.V.18		Nothing to Report	aa
ST LEGER	4.V.18		do	aa
ST LEGER	5.V.18		ditto	aa
ST LEGER	6.V.18		ditto	aa
ST LEGER	7.V.18		ditto	aa
ST LEGER	8.V.18		ditto	aa
ST LEGER	9.V.18		ditto	aa
ST LEGER	10.V.18		CAPT. W.O.L. HICKEY RAMC (TF) reported for duty	aa
ST LEGER	11.V.18		Nothing to Report	aa
ST LEGER	12.V.18		Nothing to Report	aa
ST LEGER	13.V.18		Nothing to Report	aa
ST LEGER	14.V.18		Nothing to Report	aa

Army Form C. 2118.

WAR DIARY
or
INTELLIGENCE SUMMARY.
(Erase heading not required.)

Instructions regarding War Diaries and Intelligence Summaries are contained in F. S. Regs., Part II. and the Staff Manual respectively. Title pages will be prepared in manuscript.

*[Stamp: 2nd WEST RIDING FIELD AMBULANCE * R.A.M.C.(T.) Sheet 7]*

Place	Date	Hour	Summary of Events and Information	Remarks and references to Appendices
ST LEGER	15.V.18		CAPT. G. STIELL, 1 NCO & 19 OR reported as advance party to the 49th Field Amb (37 div) at the A.D.S. BIENVILLERS for the purpose of relay post until new unit out.	RA
ST LEGER	16.V.18		CAPT G.C. JACK. 4 NCO's & 28 OR reported as advance party to the 49th Field Amb & A.D.S. BIENVILLERS with one bearer Motor Ambulance.	RA
ST LEGER	17.V.18		2 Bearer squads & one nurses attached to each of the Battalions (5th 2/4, 2/7 W.R.) & 12, 1813 pd. to Machine Gunner M.O. whilst the Division was in the line. CAPT E.M. ASHCROFT proceeded to the 62nd DIV. WING at ORVILLE for duty. MAJOR ANDERSON, 11 NCO's & 34 OR. proceeded to BIENVILLERS to take over the A.D.S. from the 49th Field Ambulance ready to be completed by 6 am on the 18th. The rest of the Motor Ambulance (less one Ford) proceeded to A.D.S. for duty. The HdQrs proceeded to HENU for use of C.O. 2 bearer motor Amb's from 4/2 W.R. 2 units & 2 from the 2/3rd also reported at the A.D.S. for S.E. The motor cars & 1 G.S. waggon with orderlies Room attached to A.D.S. The C.O. Quartermaster & rest (about together with Pan transport (less 2 motor cars + 1 G.S. waggon) proceeded to HENU & established the HdQrs there nothing over the camp at G. Chantre Rue from the H.Q.? The 49th Field Amb. HdQrs, officers & personnel being accommodated in Tents.	RA

Army Form C. 2118.

WAR DIARY
or
INTELLIGENCE SUMMARY.
(Erase heading not required.)

Instructions regarding War Diaries and Intelligence Summaries are contained in F. S. Regs., Part II. and the Staff Manual respectively. Title pages will be prepared in manuscript.

*Stamp: 2/2nd WEST RIDING FIELD AMBULANCE * R.A.M.C. (T) — Sheet 3*

Place	Date	Hour	Summary of Events and Information	Remarks and references to Appendices
HENU BIENVILLERS	18.v.18		The ADS at BIENVILLERS, + relay posts are opened. Area taken over + relay/employés by 6 a.m. for screens & examination from forward area are attached appendix. CAPT SHARRAD RAMC (TF) 2/3 W.R. Fld Amb reports to the ADS for duty together with 2 NCO's + 28 other ranks from H.Q. 2/3 W.R.T. Amb. New draught Bergman from FONQUEVILLERS	APPENDIX "A" aa
HENU	19.v.18		Work in increasing protection of ADS against bombs by Sandbagging etc carried out. Are the relays + RAP's visited by CAPT G. STIELL as O/C Bienvers.	aa
HENU	20.v.18		CAPT FREW RAMC of the 2/3 W.R. Fld Amb reports to the unit for duty. 5 NCO's + 28 OR of the 2/1 W.R.T. Amb reports for duty at the ADS	aa
HENU	21.v.18		Nothing to report	aa
HENU	22.v.18		Our M.O. (LIEUT BASSETT) opened at FONQUEVILLERS. Coa Rolling Post where enlargement + protective construction work is being carried out under orders & purview of the R.E. WILLOW PATCH TRACK being used "walking wounded" squads, stretcher post started commenced at the junction of the WILLOW PATCH TRACK with the BIENVILLERS — SOUASTRE ROAD for refreshment + rest of walking wounded.	aa
HENU	23.v.18		2 NCO's + 60 OR (Bandsmen) from Infantry battalion of the Division reports to ADS for duty at Stretcher Bearers. A party from base squad sent to Relay Post to cater a RAMC Screen. So we at Bruen Sq'd at the Relay Post is now made up of 2 officers & 2 RAMC Bruen	aa

T2134. Wt. W708—776. 500000. 4/15. Sir J. C. & S.

Army Form C. 2118.

WAR DIARY
or
INTELLIGENCE SUMMARY.
(Erase heading not required.)

Instructions regarding War Diaries and Intelligence Summaries are contained in F. S. Regs., Part II. and the Staff Manual respectively. Title pages will be prepared in manuscript.

2/2nd WEST RIDING FIELD AMBULANCE — *R.A.M.C. (T)* — Sheet 4

Place	Date	Hour	Summary of Events and Information	Remarks and references to Appendices
HENU	24.V.18		Motor Amb. loading stations at the car park at HANNESCAMPS withdrawn during the Raid in very early morning for shelter & shortly afterwards returned. Construction work still being carried out at the loading post (Browery Post) at FONQUEVILLERS & the bathing-room D.I. Section at the C.B. The WILLOW PATCH TRACK A.D.S.	
HENU	25.V.18		Whole of R/AMC personnel in forward Relay Post relieved & brought back to ADS. The various construction works still being carried out.	
HENU	26.V.18		Nothing to Report.	
HENU	27.V.18		A dug-out shelter commenced to be constructed at E.16.c.2.6 just off the WILLOW PATCH TRACK west of the Orchard on the HANNESCAMPS — FONQUEVILLERS ROAD near entrance to the Post at FONQUEVILLERS ADS namely the temporary dressing down the WILLOW PATCH TRACK from "Z" Post.	
HENU	28.V.18		The dug-out shelter near the ORCHARD carried on with. Blockhouse roofing approximately 22ft x 8ft other works still going on.	
HENU	29.V.18		Car control & car park for Motor Ambulances (Batt. Level ADS & one at FONQUEVILLERS) established at the BRICKWORKS (E.7.d.2.8) on the BENVILLERS — SOUASTRE ROAD. The various construction works still going on. Horse Battle at ADS strength intake on bays & bedding.	

WAR DIARY
or
INTELLIGENCE SUMMARY.

Army Form C. 2118.

Place	Date	Hour	Summary of Events and Information	Remarks and references to Appendices
HENU	30.V.18		Further construction work being done at the end of the WILLOW PATCH TRACK in the BIENVILLERS — SOUASTRE ROAD another emplacement being constructed for the accommodation of walking wounded. A shelter for a Light Motor Ambulance also being constructed at the bottom of the bank below Z. post on LA BRAYELLE FARM ROAD as a car loading post from the Car to carry Patients from Post "Z" to either "COLONEL'S WALK", where is situated post in front of FONQUEVILLERS, or direct to Car loading Post at either FONQUEVILLERS or the Supermarine Ho. ORCHARD.	
HENU	31.V.18		"Z" Post & 92 BIENVILLERS on the BIENVILLERS — SOUASTRE ROAD had another ? type of the previous construction — a double Elephant hut protection another for protecting stretcher cases, & also the post sitters, and is Fortified lately & an annexe by a Rolling Fort. Further improvement on other R.A.P. on the various construction work was being carried out during day. Various shelters at FONQUEVILLERS (day aid & am night & pm) made Progress in work of construction.	

Lieut. Colonel R.A.M.C. (T)
Commanding ... Field Ambulance.

A. Andrew
Major R.A.M.C.

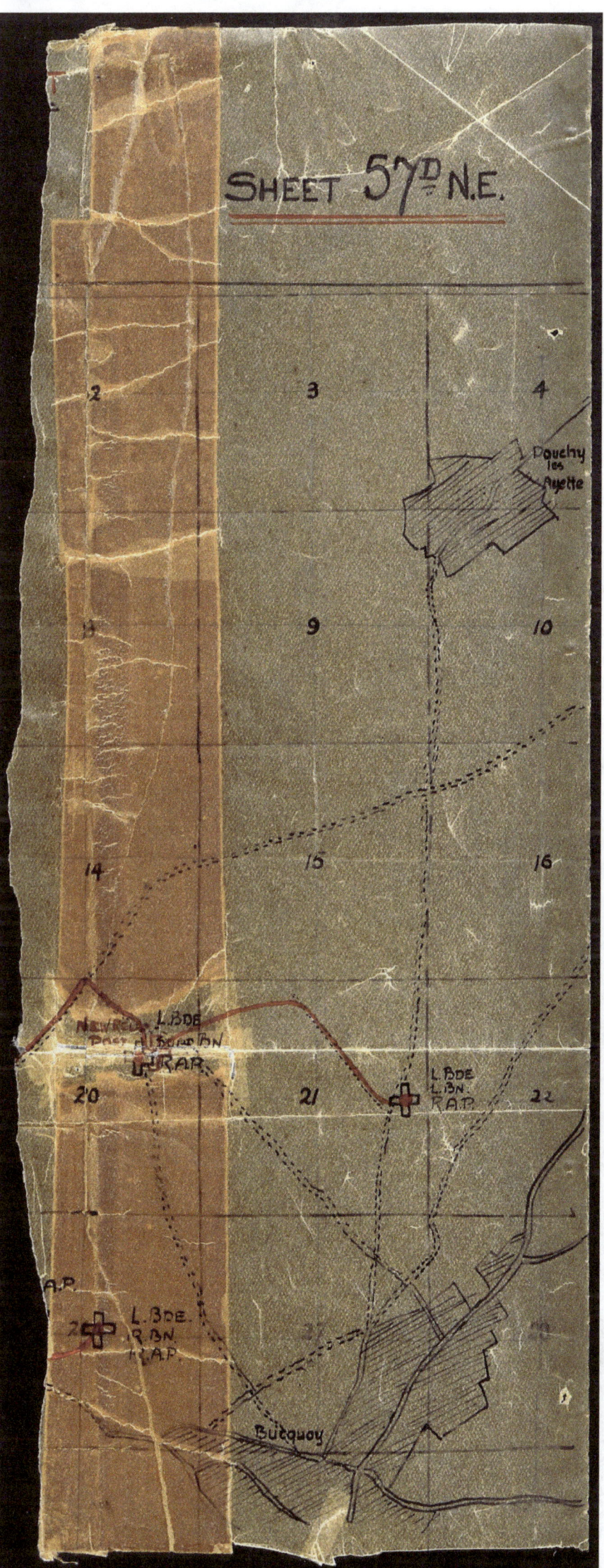

APPENDIX "A"

"Scheme for the Evacuation of the Forward Area"

Main Dressing Station at Souastre 2/1 W.R. Field Amb
A.D.S. at BIENVILLERS & forward area in charge of O.C. 2/2
W.R. Field Amb.

There are 4 forward R.A.P's & 3 SUPPORT R.A.P's to evacuate from, these may roughly be represented as a RIGHT & LEFT forward Battalion in a RIGHT & LEFT SECTOR with a SUPPORT Battalion behind each SECTOR & a RESERVE (SUPPORT) behind the whole

```
                                    • RAP
   Reserve      Support
   • RAP        • RAP
                                    • RAP
              Support
              • RAP                 • RAP

                                    • RAP
```

The main line of evacuation of wounded is through the Right Sector (see accompanying MAP).

The Left RAP of LEFT SECTOR & its SUPPORT RAP is evacuated to a RELAY POST (HENLEY) at F.19.2.7.8 where 1 NCO & 2 squads of bearers are stationed.

The RT RAP of LT SECTOR & (L) RAP of (R) SECTOR evacuate to Relay Post "KITE COPSE" F.24.d.6.0 where 1 NCO & 3 squads are stationed.

The (R) RAP of (R) SECTOR & its SUPPORT RAP together with the RESERVE SUPPORT RAP evacuate through LA BRAYELLE FARM RELAY (E.24.c.4.4. one NCO & 4 squads) to "Z" POST E.23.d.4.6 where 2 M.O's, 2 NCOs & 6 squads are stationed, one of the officers being O/c Bearers.

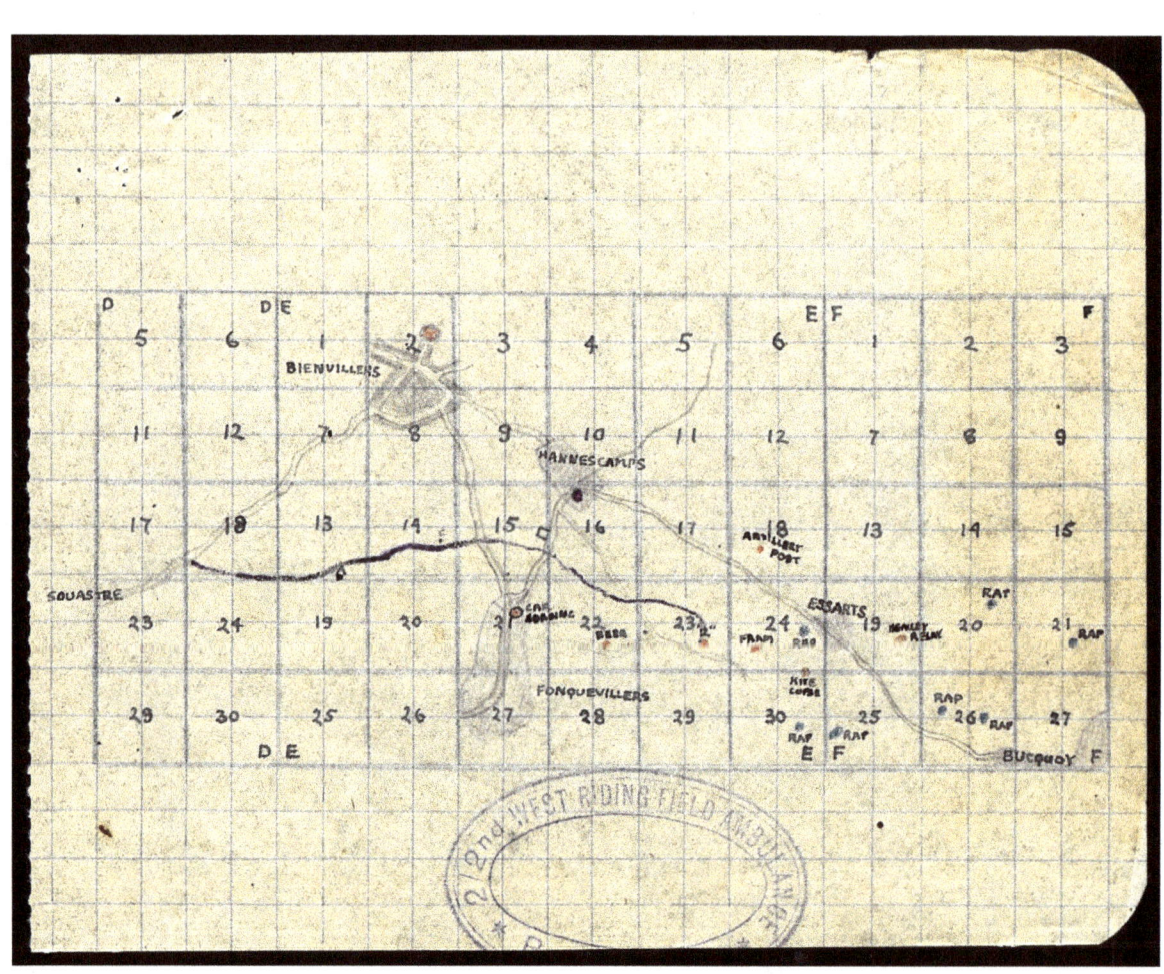

The cases collected at "Z" Relay are evacuated through a Relay post in BEER TRENCH (E22 d 2.6) on the LA BRAYELLE ROAD where 1 NCO + 4 squads are stationed to the "car loading post" (BREWERY POST) in FONQUEVILLERS where 1 M.O. 1NCO + 2 squads together with one (often 2) Motor Ambulances are stationed.

An additional post is held for the artillery by one squad in the QUARRY (ARTILLERY POST) at E18 c 6.5 with Relay Post at E16 a 6.9 HANNESCAMPS where one squad is stationed with 2 pairs wheeled stretcher carriers (formerly one Motor Ambulance), these evacuate down the HANNESCAMPS — BIENVILLERS ROAD to A.D.S. (E 2 d 5.8) BIENVILLERS to which point also the Motor Ambulances stationed at FONQUEVILLERS clear, coming down the FONQUEVILLERS — BIENVILLERS ROAD.

Owing to a change in position of the (L) Batt. ~~SUPPORT~~ RAP, Left Bdl, an additional Relay Post is under construction at a point in BRADFORD TRENCH, viz F.20 B.5.4 The work was commenced on 27/5/18.

31 V 18

A. Anderson
Major R.A.M.C.(T)

APPENDIX "B"

SUPPLEMENTARY ROUTE from "Z" Post

For Walking Wounded & if necessary Stretcher cases. By overland track in a N.W. direction through E.23.a crossing the HANNESCAMPS — POPLAR ROAD at E.16.d.4.2 where it joins the dry weather "WILLOW PATCH" TRACK to SOUASTRE — BIENVILLERS ROAD, which crosses the HANNESCAMPS — FONQUEVILLERS ROAD just SOUTH of the ORCHARD, thence across the FONQUEVILLERS — BIENVILLERS ROAD past WILLOW PATCH "C", past WILLOW PATCH "A" joining the BIENVILLERS — SOUASTRE ROAD at point D.17.d.8.2.

Relays as follows :— one in trench at E.16.d.4.2 another large dug-out with "Elephant" shrapnel proof cover in trench just south of the "ORCHARD", next relay WILLOW PATCH "C" then WILLOW PATCH "A" & at the termination of the track on the BIENVILLERS — SOUASTRE ROAD a covered shelter where nourishment can be given & wounds seen to, an M.O & bearers being stationed there. Thence by road to M.D.S at SOUASTRE.

This scheme may be amplified so as to occlude BIENVILLERS, by further strengthening the personnel at the post near the ORCHARD & also the post at the end of the WILLOW PATCH TRACK on the BIENVILLERS — SOUASTRE ROAD, also a CAR LOADING POST is being provided at the bottom of the hill below "Z" Post on LA BRAYELLE ROAD for a FORD MOTOR AMBULANCE to carry patients from below "Z" post to either COLONEL'S WALK which is at point E21 C.9.4 just in front of FONQUEVILLERS or direct down to car loading post at either FONQUEVILLERS or the ORCHARD

A. Anderson
Major R/AMC(T)

MEDICAL

ORIGINAL Vol 18
140/30/6.

Confidential
War Diary
of
2/2nd W.R. Field Ambulance

From 1st June to 30th June 1918

Volume 18.

COMMITTEE FOR THE
MEDICAL HISTORY OF ...
Date 7 AUG 1918

WAR DIARY
or
INTELLIGENCE SUMMARY.
(Erase heading not required.)

Army Form C. 2118.

Sheet 1.

Place	Date	Hour	Summary of Events and Information	Remarks and references to Appendices
HENU	1.6.18		The Unit is still responsible for clearance of the forward area with A.D.S. at BIENVILLERS & FONQUEVILLERS & Unit of evacuation as given in appendix "A". Wagon Lines & Head Quarters at HENU.	R.J.B.
HENU	2.6.18		Nothing to report	R.J.B.
HENU	3.6.18		A relief of Bearers was completed in the forward area by Bearers detached from notes at Head Quarters.	R.J.B.
HENU	4.6.18		Nothing to report	R.J.B.
HENU	5.6.18		" "	R.J.B.
HENU	6.6.18		Capt. W.J. LACEY HICKEY, R.A.M.S. (T.F.) proceeded on temporary duty to 2/7 WEST YORKS REGT as M.O. in charge.	R.J.B.
HENU	7.6.18		Nothing to report	
HENU	8.6.18		Ditto	
HENU	9.6.18		Ditto	
HENU	10.6.18		Ditto	
HENU	11.6.18		Ditto	
HENU	12.6.18		Ditto	R.J.B.

Army Form C. 2118.

Sheet 2

WAR DIARY
or
INTELLIGENCE SUMMARY.
(Erase heading not required.)

Instructions regarding War Diaries and Intelligence Summaries are contained in F. S. Regs., Part II. and the Staff Manual respectively. Title pages will be prepared in manuscript.

Place	Date	Hour	Summary of Events and Information	Remarks and references to Appendices
HENU	13.6.18		A relief of the bearers on the forward mis. was completed by stress who had been rested	R.J.B.
HENU	14.6.18		nothing to report	R.J.B.
HENU	15.6.18		MAJOR A. ANDERSON R.A.M.C. (T.F.) proceeded on 14 days ordinary leave to UNITED KINGDOM.	R.J.B.
			CAPT. SHARRARD R.A.M.C. from 2/3 W.R.F. Amb a Mules temporarily to the Unit reported to 49 Fm. U.S.I. for temporary duty on N.O.P. 15.6.18.	R.J.B.
			18 O.R. 2/7 West.York. Reg. attached to this Unit as Stretcher bearers were relieved by 18 O.R. of 1/5 DEVON Regt.	
			8 O.R. 3 WEST RIDING Regt. reported to A.D.S. DIENVILLERS in relief of a similar number of 2/7 WEST RIDING REGT.	R.J.B.
HENU	16.6.18		CAPT. W.J. LACEY HICKEY R.A.M.C. (T.F.) returned from temp. Duty with the 2/7 WEST.YD.RIS. REGT. 16.4.18	R.J.B.
HENU	17.6.18		nothing to report	R.J.B.
HENU	18.6.18		nothing to report	R.J.B.
HENU	19.6.18		A relief of bearers at the forward posts was completed by bearers who	

Army Form C. 2118.

Sheet 3

WAR DIARY
or
INTELLIGENCE SUMMARY.
(Erase heading not required.)

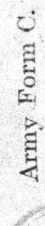

Place	Date	Hour	Summary of Events and Information	Remarks and references to Appendices
HENU	19.6.18		had been resting at Head Quarters	
			A relief was carried out of 9 O.R. attached 2/4 WEST RIDING REGT. R.A.P. & 9 O.R. attached 2/4 HANTS REGT. R.A.P.	
HENU.	20.6.18		During the night 20.6.18 HENLEY RELAY POST 5-7. D. F.19.D.7.8. was thrown in by a direct hit from an enemy shell 1 N.C.O. & 2 men R.A.M.C. being killed. R.Y.B.	
HENU.	21.6.18		Lieut. S.H. OSBORNE M.O. 129 U.S.A. reported & was taken on strength of this Unit. R.Y.B.	
HENU.	22.6.18		CAPT. ASHCROFT R.A.M.S. (T.C.) was taken off the strength of this Unit & proceeded to report to M.O. i/c 62 Divn. R.E.'s	88/13
HENU.	23.6.18		CAPT. W.T. LACEY. HICKEY. R.A.M.S. (T.F.) posted as permanent M.O. i/c 2/4 WEST RIDING REGT. & was taken on the strength of this Unit. R.Y.B.	
HENU.	24.6.18		On night of 23rd/24th. 26 O.R. A/E W.R.F. and. were relieved. Ankle turned over and returned to their Unit. 24th inst.	R.Y.B.
			Construction of new shelter on the Bruyelle Rd. commenced at 57.D. E.22. C.7.4. to accommodate squads from La Bruyelle P. Relay. E.22. D.8.3. who had to come back.	R.Y.B.
HENU.	25.6.18		The 3-D Field Amb. relieved this Unit in the RIGHT SECTOR of the	

T2134. Wt. W708-776. 500000. 4/15. Sir J. C. & S.

WAR DIARY
or
INTELLIGENCE SUMMARY.

Army Form C. 2118.

Sheet 4.

Place	Date	Hour	Summary of Events and Information	Remarks and references to Appendices
HENU	25.6.18		(carried over on the night of 24/25 - cont.)	R.J.B.
HENU	26.6.18		The personnel of the S.D.S. Field Amb. relieved the personnel of the 2nd 2A Field Amb. bearers in the LEFT SECTOR on night of 25/26.R. The following accompanied the bearer units: 4 M.R. 2/4 W.R. Regt — 13 C.R. 3-4 W.R. Regt — 6 C.R. K.O.Y.L.I. — 7 C.R. 2/4 Yorkies — 18 C.R. 1/5 Devons — 6 C.R. S.KOYLI from A.D.S. BIENVILLERS. R.J.B. The S.D.S Field Amb. completed relief of this unit at the A.D.S. BIENVILLERS & FONQUEVILLERS & took over the evacuation of the forward area. The personnel of this unit & attached those still attached concentrated at HENU. 3-7 D. D19. L.3.6. — The Head Quarters of this Unit moved from D19.L-8.6. 52B HENU to D19.L.7.2. 57 D. & opened a small hospital for treatment of the sick of 187 Inf. Bde. & 186 Inf. Bde. The hospital composed of Bells & canvas.	R.J.B.
HENU	27.6.18		2.6 C.R. 2/1. W. R. 4. Amb. rejoined their Units 27/6/18	R.J.B
HENU	28.6.18		nothing to report.	R.J.A

Army Form C. 2118.

Sheet 5

WAR DIARY
or
INTELLIGENCE SUMMARY.
(Erase heading not required.)

Instructions regarding War Diaries and Intelligence Summaries are contained in F. S. Regs., Part II. and the Staff Manual respectively. Title pages will be prepared in manuscript.

Place	Date	Hour	Summary of Events and Information	Remarks and references to Appendices
HENU	29.6.18		Nothing to report	R.J.B
HENU	30.6.18		Nothing to report.	R.J.B

R J Booth Lieut R.A.M.C

C. Ward
Lieut. Colonel, R.A.M.C.(T.F.)
Commanding 2/2nd W.R. Field Ambulance.

APPENDIX A

Disposition of Area shared by 2/1, 2/2 & 2/3 N.R. 2 Amb.

TITLE OF POST	DESCRIPTION	MAP REFERENCE	PERSONNEL OFFICERS	PERSONNEL N.C.O.s	PERSONNEL MEN	VEHICLES	WHEELED STRETCHER CARRIERS	STRETCHERS	BLANKETS	PETROL TINS FOR WATER	REMARKS
R.A.P. Left Bde. Left Bn.	Trp Trench – Shallow dugout	F.21.a.7.8.			9						2 Squads & 1 sturcher
do — Right Bn.	Subway Road splinter proof shelter	F.20.d.5.5.			9						—do—
do — Supp. Bn.	Essarts Deep Dugout	E.24.d.6.9.			9						—do—
R.A.P. Right Bde. Left Bn.	Camouflage Trench splinter proof shelter	F.2b.a.5.1.			9		2				—do—
do — Right Bn.	Rettemoy Farm Reinforced cellars	F.25.c.0.7.			9						—do—
do — Supp. Bn.	Pigeon Wood Bat. H.Q.	E.29.b.9.6.			9						—do—
R.A.P. Reserve Bde. 1st Bn.	Battn. H.Q.	E.23.c.6.5.			9						—do—
do — 2nd Bn.	—do—	Souastre			9						—do—
do — 3rd Bn.	—do—	—do—			9						—do—
NEW RELAY	Shallow Dugout	F.20.b.5.4.			8		1	4	8	3	Blown up & out of use
HENLEY RELAY	Splinter Proof Shelter (Blown in)	F.19.d.7.8.			4						Temporary
PILL BOX RELAY	Essart's Cemetery German Pill Box	F.19.c.8.2.			4						
KITE COPSE RELAY	Dugout	E.24.D.b.0.		1 Sgt.	12		3	17	30	6	
FARM RELAY	—do—	E.24.c.4.4.			4		1	1	11	2	
"Z" RELAY	—do—	E.23.D.4.6.	1	1 Cpl. 1 Sgt.	19		3	17	53	10	
LA BRAYELLE RD. RELAY	Splinter troop Shelter	E.22.D.2.5.		1 Cpl.	16		3	4	27	6	There is a new shelter dug out in process of making at E.22.c.9.4
ARTILLERY POST RELAY	Dugout	E.19.c.6.5.			4			1	2		
HANNESCAMPS POST	Reinforced cellar	E.10.c.6.0.		1 Sgt. 1 Cpl.	4						Loading Post.
A.D.S. FONQUEVILLERS	Elephant Shelters and cellars	E.21.b.1.1.	1	1 Cpl.	13	1 Daimler Ambce.		21	25	26	
A.D.S. BIENVILLERS	House - sandbagged	E.2.D.5.8.	3	5 Sgts 3Cpls 9 L/C	103	1 Daimler 4 Ambces					
ORCHARD DUGOUT	Elephant Shelter	E.16.c.1.b.			2			1	2		Holding Posts.
WILLOW PATCH SHACK	Shelters (2) Sandbagged	D.18.c.8.8.			2						Holding Party.

MEDICAL

Vol 19
140/3131.

Confidential
War Diary
of
2/2nds West Riding Field Ambce.

From 1st July To 31st July 1918

Volume 19

COMMITTEE FOR THE
MEDICAL HISTORY OF THE WAR
Date 6 SEP 1916

ORIGINAL
July 1918

WAR DIARY
or
INTELLIGENCE SUMMARY.

(Erase heading not required.)

Army Form C. 2118.

MEDICAL

Place	Date	Hour	Summary of Events and Information	Remarks and references to Appendices
HENU	1/7/18		Unit in rest billets evacuating sick of 186 Inf Brigade	Columns
HENU	2/7/18		MAJOR A ANDERSON R.A.M.C(T.F) returned from 14 days leave in U.K.	CWP
HENU	3/7/18		Nothing to report.	CWP
HENU	4/7/18		1 N.C.O & 110/R returned back for duty from the 3rd Canadian Stationary Hospital.	CWP
HENU	5/7/18		Nothing to report.	CWP
HENU	6/7/18		MAJOR G. STELL R.A.M.C(T.S.) proceeded to No 3 C.C.S for a course on Blood transfusion.	L.W.P. CWP
HENU	6/7/18		Nothing to report	CWP
HENU	7/7/18		Nothing to report.	CWP
HENU	8/7/18		Nothing to report	CWP
HENU	9.7.18		Nothing to Report.	C.Andrew
HENU	10.7.18		The ADMS inspected the Unit (Personnel & Transport A.S.C - MT) all available men & vehicles were on parade, after the inspection the available Field Amb Site were gone through, with a few minor points for discussion. Amb in column of Route	aa

Army Form C. 2118.

WAR DIARY
or
INTELLIGENCE SUMMARY.
(Erase heading not required.)

Instructions regarding War Diaries and Intelligence Summaries are contained in F. S. Regs., Part II. and the Staff Manual respectively. Title pages will be prepared in manuscript.

Place	Date	Hour	Summary of Events and Information	Remarks and references to Appendices
HENU	11.7.18		Lt-Col EAMES RAMC(T) proceeded on leave to the United Kingdom for 14 days	
HENU	12.7.18		Nothing to report	
HENU	13.7.18		Unit was placed under orders to be prepared to move by Stretcher bearer. The sick of the 186 & 187 Inf Brigade were collected during night of 13/14 & 12 patients on the 7 Amb evacuated. MAJOR G STIELL returned to the unit from his course of special instruction at the No 3 C.C.S.	
HENU	14.7.18		Evacuation of Field Hospital & remaining sick of the 2 Inf Brigade completed with the help of 1D MAC cars. One officer & 2 OR left the Unit in Advance Billeting party. Two Ford cars & 1 Saunder unit driven & orderlies entrained at DOULLENS 1.30 p.m	
HENU	15.7.18		This Unit, together with the Horse Transport proceeded by road to MENDICOURT & there entrained at noon to join the XXII CORPS proceeding via DOULLENS & AMIENS	
EN ROUTE	16.7.18		Still proceeding by train via PARIS, MELUN, SENS, St FLORENTIN. Remainder of Motor Transport (4 Saunders w drivers & orderlies entrained SAULTY 1.30 am	

T2134. Wt. W708—776. 500000. 4/15. Sir J. C. & S.

Army Form C. 2118.

WAR DIARY
or
INTELLIGENCE SUMMARY.
(Erase heading not required.)

Instructions regarding War Diaries and Intelligence Summaries are contained in F. S. Regs., Part II. and the Staff Manual respectively. Title pages will be prepared in manuscript.

Place	Date	Hour	Summary of Events and Information	Remarks and references to Appendices
EN ROUTE	17/7/18		The Unit with its Rwee transport arrived at SOMMESOUS etc and detrained there at 4.30 a.m. Proceeded by route march via VATRY & CHENIERS to THIBIE where accommodation was favoring on billets for the night	
THIBIE	18/7/18		Again proceeded by road from THIBIE to ATHIS where the Unit went into billets & opened a Field Hospital for the accommodation of the Sick of the Brigade. LIEUT S.H. OSBORN M.D. R.C. USA joined the 8th WEST YORKS REGT for company duty. LT COL C.W. EAMES R.A.M.C.(T) rejoined the Unit, having been recalled from leave on the 14th inst.	
ATHIS	19/7/18		The whole of the Motor Transport, excepting the Unit orderly, is proceed to forward areas. 2 sgnrs. bearers & one runner sent to each of the three battalions in the Brigade to be attached to the respective M.O.s CAPT G.G. JACK R.A.M.C. reports to the H.Q. 186 INF BRIGADE as liaison officer together with two runners. MAJOR G. STIELL (O/C Bearers) together with 2 Bearer sub division proceeded to GERMAME the new area of the 186 Brigade. Anthony with strength 3 Bearer ambulances 30 Infantrymen from the Brigade attached as bearers to Major Stiell also 2 7cd Ca RE	

T2134. Wt. W708-776. 500000. 4/15. Sir J. C. & S.

Army Form C. 2118.

WAR DIARY
or
INTELLIGENCE SUMMARY.
(Erase heading not required.)

Instructions regarding War Diaries and Intelligence Summaries are contained in F. S. Regs., Part II. and the Staff Manual respectively. Title pages will be prepared in manuscript.

Place	Date	Hour	Summary of Events and Information	Remarks and references to Appendices
ATHIS	19.7.18		LIEUT. G.M. CRAWFORD. R.A.M.C (T.C) proceeded to 622 the Con Camp at TOURS for duty. The remainder of the Unit together with M.T & Horse Transport proceeded by road to MAREUIL arriving about noon. at 5 pm received further orders & proceeded to CHAMPILLON where the unit went into billets. MAJOR G. STIELL & Brance party proceeded further forward from GERMAME to COURTAGNON LIEUT CROSSMAN. M.R.C. USA & CAPT ASHCROFT R/A.M.C (T.C) reported to this unit & proceeded to the 2/1 N.R. Field Ambc for duty at the M.D.S.	
CHAMPILLON	20.7.18		The Unit opened a WALKING WOUNDED STATION at CHAMPILLON the cases being evacuated by motor lorry to SEZANNE. Also the barouche motor Ambulance reports to M.D.S. for work together forming one Ford car returned to the unit.	
CHAMPILLON	21.7.18		One Ford ambulance proceeded to St IMOGES for duty at the M.D.S. there 18 other ranks proceeded to Major Stiells party as reliefs, which party took up its head quarters at ECUEIL FARM LIEUT R.J. BASSETT R.A.M.C (T.C) proceeded to 2/L HANTS REGT for duty as M.O. East of and side of CHAMPILLON	

Army Form C. 2118.

WAR DIARY
or
INTELLIGENCE SUMMARY.
(Erase heading not required.)

Instructions regarding War Diaries and Intelligence Summaries are contained in F.S. Regs., Part II. and the Staff Manual respectively. Title pages will be prepared in manuscript.

Place	Date	Hour	Summary of Events and Information	Remarks and references to Appendices
CHAMPILLON	22.7.18		Nothing to Report	RA
CHAMPILLON	23.7.18		Nothing to Report	RA
CHAMPILLON	24.7.18		This unit together with the 2/1 Highland Field Amb (51st Div) opened a joint WALKING WOUNDED STATION at BELLEVUE for prisoners of the 51st & 62nd Divs each keeping own divisional A-D book. Cases evacuated by lorry. MAJOR G. STELL wounded at ECUEIL FARM & evacuated to C.C.S. through the 2/1st W.R. Field Amb. M.D.S.	RA RA
CHAMPILLON	25.7.18		Nothing to Report	RA
CHAMPILLON	26.7.18		Nothing to Report	RA
CHAMPILLON	27.7.18		Nothing to Report	RA
CHAMPILLON	28.7.18		The joint WALKING WOUNDED STATION (51st & 62nd Div) closed at BELLEVUE & opened up at NANTEUIL. The remainder of the unit proceeded from CHAMPILLON to take up its headquarters at ST IMOGES	RA RA
ST IMOGES	29.7.18		Nothing to Report	RA
ST IMOGES	30.7.18		CAPT G.G. JACK & Bearer sub-division from the forward area returned to the unit. Together with the Horse Ambulance & all motor ambulances	RA

Army Form C. 2118.

WAR DIARY
or
INTELLIGENCE SUMMARY.
(Erase heading not required.)

Instructions regarding War Diaries and Intelligence Summaries are contained in F. S. Regs., Part II. and the Staff Manual respectively. Title pages will be prepared in manuscript.

Place	Date	Hour	Summary of Events and Information	Remarks and references to Appendices
ST IMOGES	31.7.18		The First ambulance attached to 2/1 W.R.F. Amb. at M.D.S returned to their unit, also the Ford ambulances employed at the WALKING WOUNDED STATION. Ammunition originally with the 2/1 Highland F Amb. (5rd Div.) & the squad attached to the M.D.S. of the Battalion of the 186 Brigade together with their ammunition stand to the unit. The infantrymen attached for duty as bearers in the forward area also returned to their respective units	AA

A. Anderson
Major R/mc(1)

C. W. Clarks
Lieut. Colonel, R.A.M.C.(T)
Commanding. 2/2nd W.R. Field Ambulance.

T2134. Wt. W708—776. 500000. 4/15. Sir J. C. & S.

MEDICAL.

Confidential.

Vol 20
140/3700

War Diary of

2/2nd W. R. Field Ambulance.

from 1st Aug: 1918 to 31st Aug 1918.

Volume 21.

COMMITTEE FOR THE
MEDICAL HISTORY OF THE WAR
Date 5 OCT. 1918

2/2ND WEST RIDING
FIELD AMBULANCE,
R.A.M.C.
No.
Date

Army Form C. 2118.

WAR DIARY
or
INTELLIGENCE SUMMARY.

(Erase heading not required.)

Instructions regarding War Diaries and Intelligence Summaries are contained in F. S. Regs., Part II. and the Staff Manual respectively. Title pages will be prepared in manuscript.

Place	Date	Hour	Summary of Events and Information	Remarks and references to Appendices
ST. IMOGES	1. VIII. 18.		The Unit with it's transport proceeded by road to CHOUILLY going on the way with the 186 Brigade when the whole Brigade moved past General BERTHELOT (the French Army Commander) at a point on the road entering into DIZY MAGENTA. The Unit bivouacked for the night on the outskirts of CHOUILLY C/town	
CHOUILLY	2. VIII 18		Nothing to Report	
CHOUILLY	3. VIII. 18		Nothing to Report	
CHOUILLY	4. VIII 18.		The Unit marched to EPERNAY where it was entraining for DOULLENS spending the night on the train.	
IN TRAIN	5. VIII 18		Passed through PARIS & AMIENS arriving DOULLENS 9.0 p.m when detraining took place & the unit marched then to MARIEUX WOOD where the IV CORPS COLLECTING STATION was taken over from the 89th FIELD AMBULANCE (63RD DIV)	
MARIEUX WOOD	6. VIII 18		LIEUT L A ANDERSON MORC USA & LIEUT A B NEVLING MORC USA reported for duty	
MARIEUX WOOD	7. VIII 18		Nothing to Report	
MARIEUX WOOD	8. VIII 18		Nothing to Report	
MARIEUX WOOD	9. VIII 18		Nothing to Report	
MARIEUX WOOD	10. VIII 18		Nothing to Report	

Army Form C. 2118.

WAR DIARY
or
INTELLIGENCE SUMMARY.
(Erase heading not required.)

Instructions regarding War Diaries and Intelligence Summaries are contained in F. S. Regs., Part II. and the Staff Manual respectively. Title pages will be prepared in manuscript.

2/2ND WEST RIDING FIELD AMBULANCE, R.A.M.C.

Place	Date	Hour	Summary of Events and Information	Remarks and references to Appendices
MARIEUX WOOD	11. VIII. 18		LT. COL C.W. EAMES proceeded on leave to the U.K. (11 days) 12 – 23rd Aug.	RE
MARIEUX WOOD	12. VIII. 18		Nothing to Report	RE
MARIEUX WOOD	13. VIII. 18		do	RE
MARIEUX WOOD	14. VIII. 18		do	RE
MARIEUX	15. VIII. 18		do	RE
MARIEUX	16. VIII. 18		do	RE
MARIEUX	17. VIII. 18		do	RE
MARIEUX	18. VIII. 18		LIEUT. S.H. OSBORNE M.O.R.C. U.S.A. reported for duty with the unit	RE
MARIEUX	19. VIII. 18		CAPT. A.M. DAVIE R.A.M.C. reported to the unit for duty. The Hospital at MARIEUX WOOD was handed over to the 1st N.Z. FIELD AMB & the unit proceeded by road with its transport to SAULTY where it was billeted in huts.	RE
SAULTY	20. VIII. 18		Nothing to Report	RE
SAULTY	21. VIII. 18		The Camp att. was handed over to the 2/3 LONDON FIELD AMB & the unit proceeded by road to THIÉVRES where it went into Billets.	RE
THIÉVRES	22. VIII. 18		LIEUT. S.H. OSBORNE M.O.R.C. U.S.A. proceeded to the 1/5 DEVONS Battalion for temporary duty	RE
THIÉVRES	23. VIII. 18		LIEUT. C.M. CRAWFORD R.A.M.C. (T.F.) proceeded to the 61st DIV. D.A.C for temporary duty	RE

Army Form C. 2118.

22ND WEST RIDING
FIELD AMBULANCE
R.A.M.C.

WAR DIARY
or
INTELLIGENCE SUMMARY.
(Erase heading not required.)

Instructions regarding War Diaries and Intelligence Summaries are contained in F.S. Regs., Part II. and the Staff Manual respectively. Title pages will be prepared in manuscript.

Place	Date	Hour	Summary of Events and Information	Remarks and references to Appendices
THIEVRES	23 VIII 18		The unit proceeded by road to SAULTY where it went into billets for the night.	
SAULTY	24 VIII 18		The unit marched with 186 Brigade transport to the outskirts of AYETTE where it bivouaced in a field on the AYETTE - COURCELLES ROAD. CAPT G G JACK RAMC with two runners was attached to the 186 Bde H.Q. Two squads of Bearers & one runner were attached to each of the Battalion M.O.'s of the 186 Brigade	
AYETTE	25 VIII 18		Lieut COL C.W. EAMES RAMC(T) returned to the unit from leave to the U.K. LIEUT A.B NEVLING MORC USA with one tent-subdivision proceeded to the M.D.S. AYETTE for temporary duty with the 5th FIELD AMB (2nd DIV) One complete Bearer subdivision together with 20 attached Infantry of 186 Bde (Bearers) reported at the A.D.S. COURCELLES for temporary duty with the 2/1 WEST RIDING FIELD AMB LIEUT L.A ANDERSON MORC USA proceeded to the 5th W.R. Regt for temporary duty as M.O.	
AYETTE	26 VIII 18		The unit took over the M.D.S. at AYETTE from the 5th FIELD AMB. at the same time a WALKING WOUNDED COLLECTING POST was established near to COURCELLES on the AYETTE - COURCELLES ROAD where 2 NCO's, 4 men were placed in charge. MAJOR SNEDDON together with one tent subdivision reported at the M.D.S for duty from the 2/3 W.R. Fd Amb Three motor lorries with drivers were attached from 30 MAC for duty to convey the	

T2134. Wt. W708—776. 500000. 4/15. Sir J. C. & S.

Army Form C. 2118.

WAR DIARY
or
INTELLIGENCE SUMMARY.
(Erase heading not required.)

Instructions regarding War Diaries and Intelligence Summaries are contained in F.S. Regs., Part II. and the Staff Manual respectively. Title pages will be prepared in manuscript.

Place	Date	Hour	Summary of Events and Information	Remarks and references to Appendices
AYETTE	26. VIII. 18.		Walking Wounded & Sick to entraining point. Two clerks were attached to H.Q. VI Corps WALKING WOUNDED COLLECTING STATION for temporary duty to replace 62nd Div A.D. book	a.
AYETTE	27 VIII 18.		Nothing to Report	a.
AYETTE	28. VIII 18.		Nothing to Report	a.
AYETTE	29. VIII 18		LIEUT L.A. ANDERSON MORC USA returned to his unit from temporary duty as MO with the 5th W. Riding Regt.	a.
AYETTE	30. VIII 18.		Nothing to Report	a.
AYETTE	31. VIII 18.		Nothing to Report	a.

C Anderson (?)
Major

C W Earnes
LIEUT-COL, R.A.M.C.
COMDG. 2/2nd WEST RIDING FIELD AMBULANCE

140/3259.

2/3r. West Riding F.A.

Sept. 1918.

COMMITTEE FOR THE
MEDICAL HISTORY OF THE WAR
Date 5 NOV 1919

Confidential

War Diary

of 2/2nd. West Riding Field Ambce.

from 1st Sept. 1918 to 30th Sept 1918

Volume 21.

MEDICAL

Army Form C. 2118.

2/2ND WEST
FIELD AMBU.
R.A.M.

WAR DIARY
or
INTELLIGENCE SUMMARY.
(Erase heading not required.)

Instructions regarding War Diaries and Intelligence Summaries are contained in F.S. Regs., Part II. and the Staff Manual respectively. Title pages will be prepared in manuscript.

Place	Date	Hour	Summary of Events and Information	Remarks and references to Appendices
AYETTE	1.IX.18		Still remaining as M.D.S. Nothing to Report.	aa
AYETTE	2.IX.18		Proceeded (an advance party of the Unit) to COMMIECOURT to take over the Chateau from the 2/1 W.R. Field Amb. Hon: Lt. QM NEWBOULT proceeded on 14 days leave to U.K.	aa
COMMIECOURT	3.IX.18		The remainder of the Unit & Transport proceeded to COMMIECOURT & there opened a Main Dressing Station	aa
COMMIECOURT	4.IX.18		LIEUT R.A. ANDERSON M.O.R.C. (U.S.A) proceeded for duty as M.O. to the 62nd DIV RECEPTION CAMP	aa
COMMIECOURT	5.IX.18		Nothing to Report	aa
COMMIECOURT	6.IX.18		One Complete Tent Sub-Division (Ecos Officer) proceeded to 21 C.C.S. WAVANS for temporary duty	aa
COMMIECOURT	7.IX.18		Nothing to Report	aa
COMMIECOURT	8.IX.18		LIEUT. C.M. CRAWFORD returned to this unit from temporary duty with the 62nd D.A.C.	aa
COMMIECOURT	9.IX.18		Nothing to Report	aa
COMMIECOURT	10.IX.18		CAPT A. MITCHELL (T.F.) reported to this unit for duty upon his return from leave to the U.K. LIEUT S.H. OSBORNE MORC (USA) remaining with 1/5 DEVONS as permanent M.O. & taken in front of the strength of this unit. The Unit proceeded by road to a point in front of HAPLINCOURT & there established a Main Dressing Station	aa

Army Form C. 2118.

2/2ND W. ST RIDING
FIELD AMBULANCE,

WAR DIARY
or
INTELLIGENCE SUMMARY.
(Erase heading not required.)

Instructions regarding War Diaries and Intelligence Summaries are contained in F. S. Regs., Part II. and the Staff Manual respectively. Title pages will be prepared in manuscript.

Place	Date	Hour	Summary of Events and Information	Remarks and references to Appendices
GOMMIECOURT	10.IX.18		CAPT. G.G. JACK proceeded with 2 runners to 186 Inf Brigade H.Q. as Liaison officer. 2 squads of bearers together with a number were attached to each of the Battalions of the 186 Brigade.	a.a.
HAPLINCOURT	11.IX.18		One Ford Sub-Sherwin (Gas Officer) from 2/3 W.R. Fees Amb. reported for duty. 29 OR Infantry from Battalion of 186 Brigade reported for duty as extra Bearers	a.a.
HAPLINCOURT	12.IX.18		Nothing to Report	a.a.
HAPLINCOURT	13.IX.18		Nothing to Report	a.a.
HAPLINCOURT	14.IX.18		Nothing to Report	a.a.
HAPLINCOURT	15.IX.18		Nothing to Report	a.a.
HAPLINCOURT	16.IX.18		The unit handed over the Station Blankets & dressings to the 8.º FIELD AMBULANCE upon their bearers taking over the Lines but they did not take over the site for their Main Dressing Station, the unit then proceeded by road to a point A14 just W. of COURCELLES on the COURCELLES - AYETTE ROAD & were accommodated in Bivouacs. LIEUT-COL C.W EAMES RAMC (T.F) proceeded to H.Q. 62.ᵈ Div Infantry for temporary duty as A.D.M.S.	a.a.
COURCELLES	17.IX.18		Nothing to Report	a.a.

Army Form C. 2118.

WAR DIARY
or
INTELLIGENCE SUMMARY.
(Erase heading not required.)

Instructions regarding War Diaries and Intelligence Summaries are contained in F. S. Regs., Part II. and the Staff Manual respectively. Title pages will be prepared in manuscript.

2/2ND WEST RIDING
FIELD AMBULANCE,
R.A.M.C.

Place	Date	Hour	Summary of Events and Information	Remarks and references to Appendices
COURCELLES	18.IX.18		Nothing to Report	aa
COURCELLES	19.IX.18		LIEUT. A.B. NEVLING. MORC. (USA) proceeded to the 2/4 HANTS Regt. for temporary duty as M.O.	aa
COURCELLES	20.IX.18		LIEUT. G.M. CRAWFORD. RAMC (TC) reported to the 2/4 WEST RIDING REGT. for temporary duty as M.O.	aa
COURCELLES	21.IX.18		Nothing to Report	aa
COURCELLES	22.IX.18		Nothing to Report	aa
COURCELLES	23.IX.18		Nothing to Report	aa
COURCELLES	24.IX.18		Nothing to Report	aa
COURCELLES	25.IX.18		This unit with its transport proceeded by road to a point (Map 57c I.27.c.6.3) just East of FREMICOURT where bivouced for the night. CAPT. G.G. JACK RAMC together with 2 runners reported to H.Q. 186 & Brigade HQ as liaison officer. Two bearers squads together with one runner reported to each M.O. of the Battalions in the 186 Brigade. For Infantryman from each of the Battalions of the 186 Brigade (30 in all) reported to this unit as additional bearers for use in the forward area	aa

WAR DIARY
or
INTELLIGENCE SUMMARY.
(Erase heading not required.)

Army Form C. 2118.

Instructions regarding War Diaries and Intelligence Summaries are contained in F. S. Regs., Part II. and the Staff Manual respectively. Title pages will be prepared in manuscript.

Place	Date	Hour	Summary of Events and Information	Remarks and references to Appendices
COURCELLES	25.IX.18		LIEUT G.M. CRAWFORD R.A.M.C. (T.C.) returned to the unit from duty as Temp. M.O. with the 2/4 WEST RIDING Regt. + was replaced by CAPT A. MITCHELL R.A.M.C. (T.F.) of this unit	Re
FREMICOURT	26.IX.18		Nothing to Report	Re
FREMICOURT	27.IX.18		This unit moved to RUYALCOURT + took over the MAIN DRESSING STATION from the 7° FIELD AMB. (3RD DIV) by 2 p.m. The Evacuation is being carried on by 30 M.A.C. for stretcher cases + walking wounded, the light walking wounded being conveyed by Motor Lorries to the Station at VELU. Hence by narrow gauge railway to BAPAUME + the stretcher cases + the bad walking wounded to the Broad gauge railway. Sitting wounded to C.C.S. at GREVILLERS. Two NCO's + 2 OR were stationed at the YMCA hut BAPAUME to supervise the transference of the walking wounded as they arrived there from one gauge to the other. One man (OR) was attached to the C.C.S. at GREVILLERS to see to the return of stretchers, blankets, splints etc on each returning car	PLAN attached Re

Army Form C. 2118.

WAR DIARY
or
INTELLIGENCE SUMMARY.
(Erase heading not required.)

Instructions regarding War Diaries and Intelligence Summaries are contained in F. S. Regs., Part II. and the Staff Manual respectively. Title pages will be prepared in manuscript.

2/2nd WEST RIDING FIELD AMBULANCE

Place	Date	Hour	Summary of Events and Information	Remarks and references to Appendices
FREMICOURT	27.IX.18		LIEUT. R.J. ST LOUIS MORE (USA) & LIEUT. CROSMAN MORE (USA) from 62nd DIV M.G.C. reported to this unit for duty at the M.D.S. All the unit motor & horse ambulance together with drivers orderlies reported to O.C. 2/3 W.R. Field Amb for duty in the forward area. The 30 attached Infantrymen bearers reported to O.C. 2/3 W.R. 7 Amb for duty.	aa aa
RUYALCOURT	28.IX.18		Nothing to report.	aa
RUYALCOURT	29.IX.18		Nothing to report.	aa
RUYALCOURT	30.IX.18		Nothing to report.	aa

C. Augustus Mayne
p/ LIEUT.-COL., R.A.M.C.,
COMMANDING 2/2nd WEST RIDING FIELD AMBULANCE.

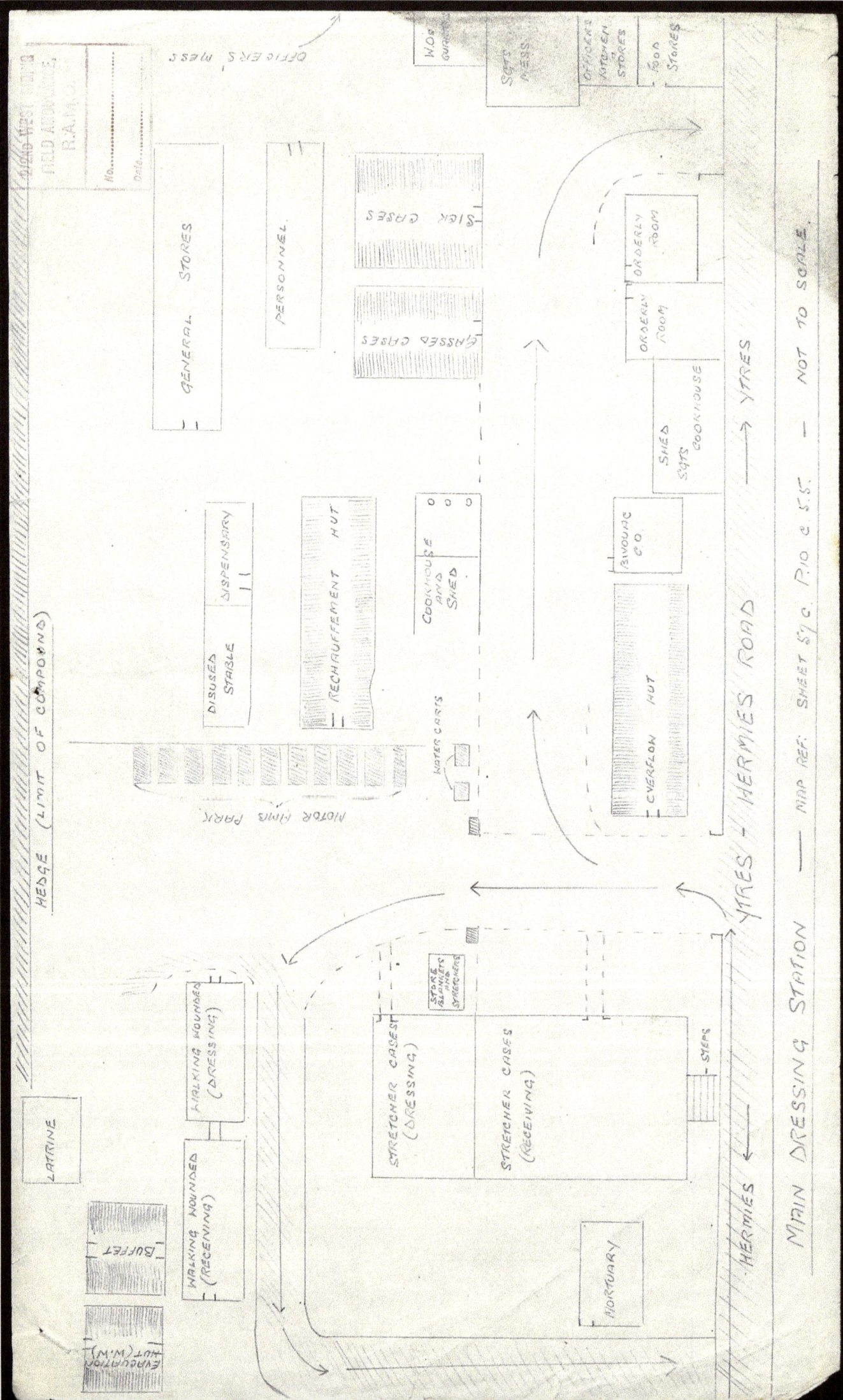

141/3327

2/2 West Riding 7 A

MEDICAL

Original

Army Form C. 2118.

Instructions regarding War Diaries and Intelligence Summaries are contained in F.S. Regs., Part II. and the Staff Manual respectively. Title pages will be prepared in manuscript.

WAR DIARY
or
INTELLIGENCE SUMMARY.
(Erase heading not required.)

ORIGINAL

2/2 8th WEST RIDING FIELD AMBULANCE

No. ....
Date ....

Place	Date	Hour	Summary of Events and Information	Remarks and references to Appendices
RUYAULCOURT	1.X.18		M.D.S. at RUYALCOURT closed at 0600 hours & opened at the same room at point K 27 d 6.6 (57c) in HAVRINCOURT CHATEAU grounds, this M.D.S. was then at 1000 hours handed over to the 7th FIELD AMB (3rd DIV) & the unit returning to RUYALCOURT as M.D.S. to liaise. CAPT C.C. JACK RAMC & several others attached to 186 Bgde HQ returned to this unit.	aa
RUYAULCOURT	2.X.18		Nothing to Report	aa
RUYAULCOURT	3.X.18		This unit together with its transport moved to point K 34 a 6.7 HAVRINCOURT where bivouacked. The 2 squads & 1 numerical attached to each battalion returning to their unit.	aa
HAVRINCOURT	4.X.18		Nothing to Report	aa
HAVRINCOURT	5.X.18		Nothing to Report	aa
HAVRINCOURT	6.X.18		Nothing to Report	aa
HAVRINCOURT	7.X.18		MAJOR A.M. DAVIE RAMC (T) proceeded on 14 days leave to the U.K.	aa
HAVRINCOURT	8.X.18		CAPT C.C. JACK RAMC together with 1 bd and divisional personnel at 2000 to RIBÉCOURT to take over the site of the evening station there from the 8th Field Amb. 2 Squads & 1 numerical what attached to each of the Battalions of the 186 Brigade & 5 Hrs. 9. D.L.I. Battalion also one numerical was attached to HQ 186 Brigade. HQ CAPT PICKLES & a Bearer Bearer sub-division reported to this unit for duty from the 2/1 W.R. Field Amb.	aa

Army Form C. 2118.

2/2nd WEST RIDING
FIELD AMBULANCE

WAR DIARY
or
INTELLIGENCE SUMMARY.
(Erase heading not required.)

Instructions regarding War Diaries and Intelligence Summaries are contained in F. S. Regs., Part II. and the Staff Manual respectively. Title pages will be prepared in manuscript.

Place	Date	Hour	Summary of Events and Information	Remarks and references to Appendices
HAVRINCOURT	9.X.18		The remainder of this unit together with its transport moved at 0600 hours to RIBECOURT & there established a COLLECTING POST, and at 1800 hours again the unit moved forward to MASNIERES & billeted for the night in a mile of pt G.2.6 & 3.7 Map 57B	
MASNIERES	10.X.18		This unit again moved forward keeping in touch with the 186 Inf Brigade upon the further advance of the enemy & proceeded to SERANVILLERS & there took over the site of the M.D.S. of GUARDS DIV H.19.5.0 & billeted there for the night	
SERANVILLERS	11.X.18		This unit again moved forward & proceeded to CARNIERES & was billeted in Rooms at pt C.13.C.3.2. CAPT PICKLES & Bearer sub division of the 2/1 W.R Field Amb returned to their own unit.	
CARNIERES	12.X.18		Nothing to Report	
CARNIERES	13.X.18		Nothing to Report	
CARNIERES	14.X.18		This unit opened a Hospital in a portion of the mill used as a M.D.S by the field division for the accommodation of sick of the 62 Div.	
CARNIERS	15.X.18		Nothing to Report	
CARNIERES	16.X.18		Nothing to Report	
CARNIERES	17.X.18		LIEUT A A SIDLL MORG (USA) reports to this unit for duty	

WAR DIARY
or
INTELLIGENCE SUMMARY.
(Erase heading not required.)

Army Form C. 2118.

Place	Date	Hour	Summary of Events and Information	Remarks and references to Appendices
CARNIERES	17.X.18		This Unit proceeded by road to QUIEVY, upon the 186 Brigade taking over part of the line held by the 62nd Division, & there established an Advanced Dressing Station at point D.14.c.0.1. in the east end of the town, whilst the Regimental Aid Post was established at the northern end of pt D.19 a 4.7. The transport (H.T.) together with Q.M. Stores stationed at BEVILLERS pt C.28. c.5.8. Method of Evacuation of Wounded APPENDIX "A" & MAP (1).	A1 MAP
QUIEVY CARNIERES	18.X.18		Nothing to Report	
QUIEVY CARNIERES	19.X.18.		LT COL C.W. EAMES RAMC(T) returning to the unit upon ceasing to perform the duties of ADMS, the ADMS being returned to the division from leave of absence. 3 Daimler motor-ambulances from the 2/1 W.R. Fd. Amb. & 2 Ford cars from H.Q. 2/3 reported to this unit for duty. Also 3 Horse ambulances each from 2/1 → 2/3. 30 Infantrymen (Bandsmen) from Battalions of the 186 Brigade reported to this unit for duty as approved Bearers in the forward area.	
QUIEVY CARNIERES	20.X.18.		Relay/post, car post & Bearers were moved forward on the battle prepared & new R.A.P.'s were established. See Appendix "B" & MAP (2).	B*MAP

WAR DIARY
or
INTELLIGENCE SUMMARY.
(Erase heading not required.)

Army Form C. 2118.

Place	Date	Hour	Summary of Events and Information	Remarks and references to Appendices
QUIEVY	21.X.18		Ambulance Car posts pushed forward as far as the Railway, & Bearers kept in touch with the various RAP's.	
QUIEVY	22.X.18		LIEUT G.M.CRAWFORD RAMC(TC) left this unit upon the termination of his contract. Various Car posts & Relays established & contact kept with various RAP's which were constantly changing. See Appendix C. + MAP (3) Prospective ADS towards SOLESMES	C
QUIEVY	23.X.18		The 3rd DIVISION passing through the 62nd, the division thus being relieved. The ADS was closed down as the Field Ambs of the 3rd Div. evacuating the forward area established their ADS in SOLESMES their MDS now being in QUIEVY. CAPT MACKENZIE RAMC(T) & Bearers of the 2/1 WR Fd Amb. together with the motor amb. & horse ambulance left this unit & returning to the 2/1. Also the motor ambulance & horse ambulance of the 2/3 returning to their own unit. The Wagon lines & Q.M Stores were now stationed at BEVILLERS moved to QUIEVY where the unit is remaining in Rest billeet.	
QUIEVY	24.X.18		MAJOR A.M DAVIE RAMC(T) returned to this unit upon the expiration of his leave.	
QUIEVY	25.X.18		The 3o attached Infantrymen (Bandsmen) from the 186 Brigade left this unit rejoining their own respective battalions. LIEUT A B NEVLING MORC (USA) was posted as MO to the 2/4 HANTS Regt.	
QUIEVY	26.X.18		The 2 Sergts & numerous attached to the MO's of the 186 Brigade returned to this unit.	

Army Form C. 2118.

WAR DIARY
or
INTELLIGENCE SUMMARY.
(Erase heading not required.)

Instructions regarding War Diaries and Intelligence Summaries are contained in F. S. Regs., Part II. and the Staff Manual respectively. Title pages will be prepared in manuscript.

Place	Date	Hour	Summary of Events and Information	Remarks and references to Appendices
QUIEVY	27 X 18		Nothing to Report	
QUIEVY	28 X 18		LIEUT A A STOLL MORC (USA) reported as temporary M.O. to 2/4 West Riding Regt	
QUIEVY	29 X 18		Nothing to Report	
QUIEVY	30 X 18		Nothing to Report	
QUIEVY	31 X 18		This Unit Fld to find guard present in the town at present in occupation were reported for 3rd DIV H.Q. This Unit H.Q. now at the MAIRE	

LIEUT.-COL. R.A.M.C.
COMDG. 2/2nd WEST RIDING FIELD AMBULANCE.

APPENDIX A.

The scheme for the evacuation of Wounded up to Zero on the 20th October 18. was as follows:-

There was only one R.A.P. in joint use by the two Battns in the line and this was situated at billet 17 on the SOLESMES road at point D.14.c.7.3. just about 100 yards away from the A.D.S. at point D.14.c.0.1. One Daimler and three Fords were stationed at the A.D.S. a car being sent up to the R.A.P. upon request. A car control post was established at point D.19.a.3.7. near the Headquarters of the unit, and whenever a car passed loaded a fresh car was sent down to the A.D.S. to take its place so that there was always a Daimler on hand for immediate use at the A.D.S. A. Walking Wounded Loading Post was established at the farm at the western end of the village (point C.24.b.3.7.) on the QUIEVY - BEVILLERS road where the whole of the horse ambulances of the Division were stationed and where a buffet was established and a Medical Officer in attendance. The Walking Wounded were collected at the A.D.S. into batches of twelve and escorted by guides to the Loading Post. The Sick also reported at the Walking Wounded Loading Post and were evacuated by Horse Ambulance.
Three hours before Zero the R.A.P's were situated as follows.

```
2/4th West Riding Regt.       D.14.c.7.3.
   th West Riding Regt.     )
2/4th York and Lancs Regt.   ) D.10.d.4.3.
```

SECRET

SHEET 1.
POSITION ZERO 20.10.18
SHEET 57B 1/40,000.

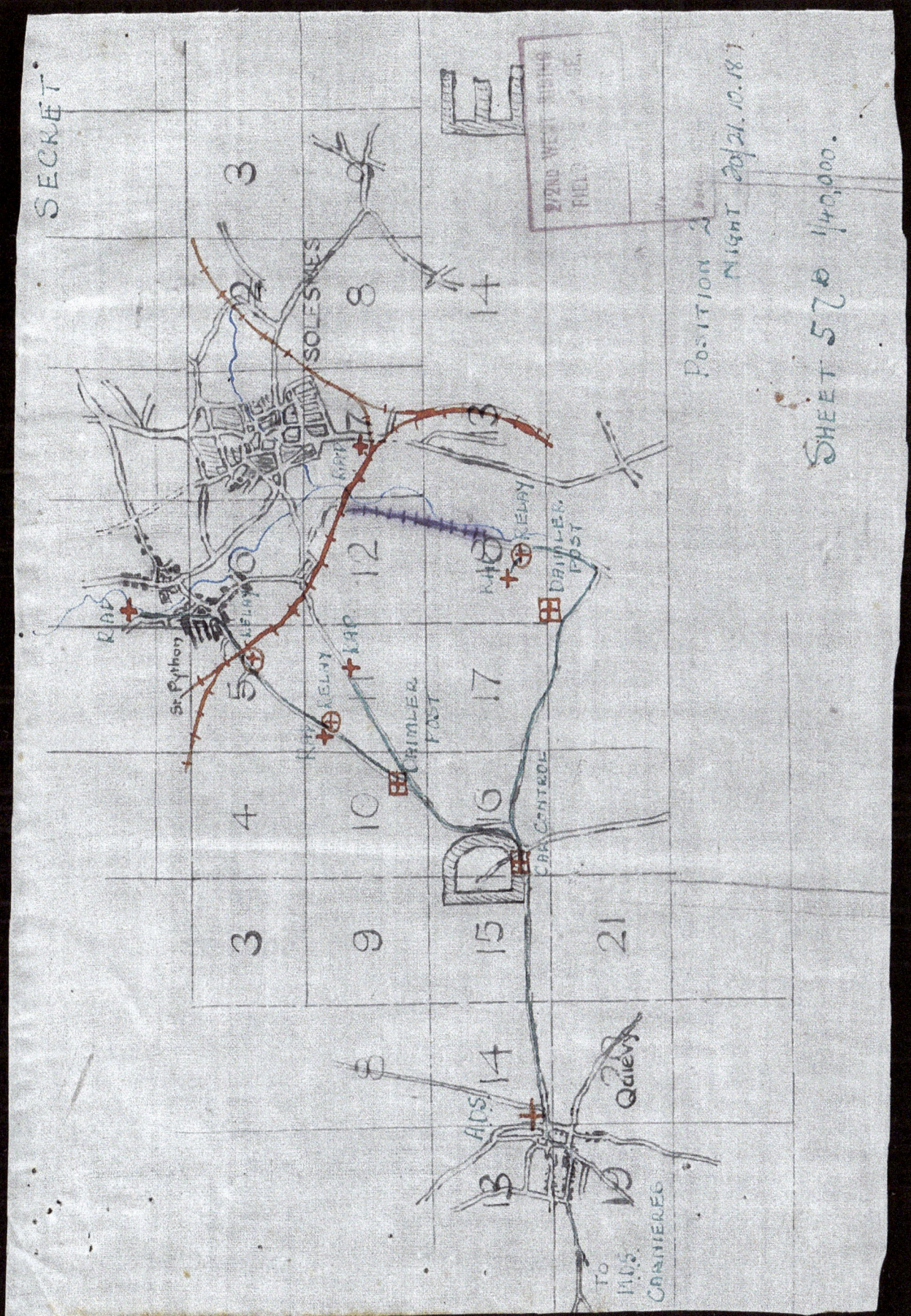

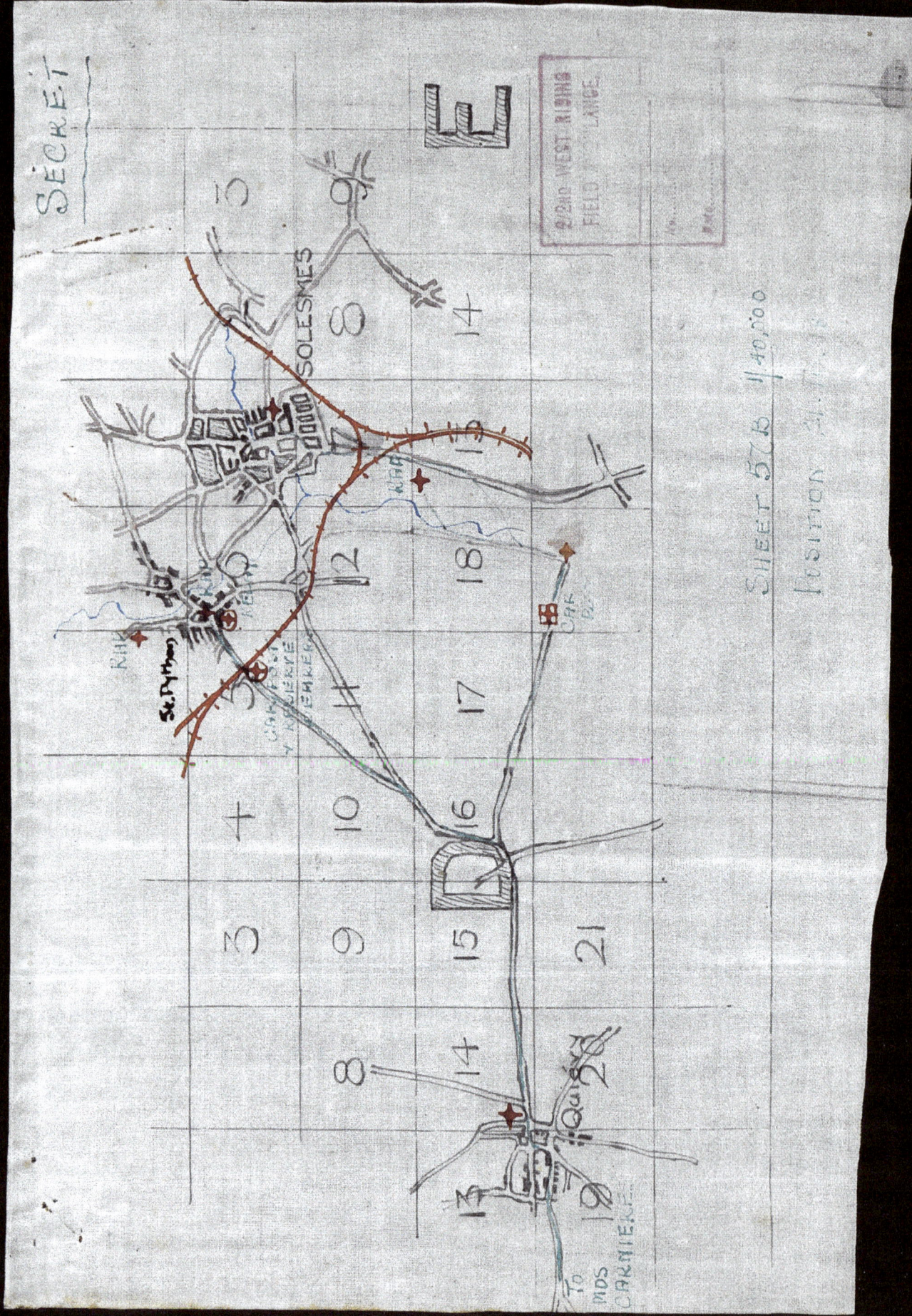

APPENDIX B

A brief outline of the scheme of attack was as follows.

The 186th Infantry Brigade and one Battn of the 187th Infantry Brigade represented the 62nd Division in the line with the 42nd Division on the Right and the Guards Division on the Left. At Zero hour the Battns were lined up along the railway running through D.5. 12. and 18. as follows

    Right Sector 2/4th York and Lancs Regt. at D.18 and D.12.d.
    Middle Sector 2/4th West Riding Regt. at D.12. a. and b.
    Left Sector in D.5.a.b.and d. 5th West Riding Regt. supported
                     by 2/4th Hants Regt.

The 2/4th West Riding Regt. had to proceed for the main central portion of SOLESMES. The 2/4th York and Lancs Regt. had to take the Railway Triangle in E.7. and the Factory afterwards clearing up the area E.7.a. D.12.b. and D.6. c. and d. behind the 2/4th West Riding Regt. Meanwhile the 5th West Riding Regt. supported by the 2/4th Hants Regt cleared ST PYTHON.
Eventually the Battns arrived through SOLESMES about the line through E.1.b. and d. and consolidated there, the 185th Infantry Brigade passing through them, the final objective being the heights beyond the town along the road running through W.20. c. and d. which were reached up to time.

Phase 1. At Zero hour the R.A.P's were as follows.
    5th West Riding Regt. and 2/4th Hants Regt. D.5.a.7.6.
    Railway Embankment.
    2/4th West Riding Regt. D.14.c.7.3. Billet 17 QUIEVY.
    2/4th York and Lancs Regt. D.18.c. 7.6. Railway Embankment
A Ford car was stationed at D.15.d.5.4. just short of the Orchard at D.16.4.5. which at this time was continually being shelled.
Another Ford Car ran as far as possible along the low road through D.16.d. meeting bearers from a Relay stationed at D.17.d.3.0. clearing the Right Sector.
Other Relays were put out along the road as follows. D.16.a.7.1. and D.10.d.4.3. where there was a house with a good cellar at the fork of the road. The Middle Sector was cleared through a Bearer Relay Post stationed at D.11.b.0.2. The Left Sector through Bearer Relay posts at D.11.a.4.8. and D.5.d.0.4.

Phase 2. As the attack proceeded a Daimler car replaced the Ford Car at D.15.d.5.4. A Ford car was pushed forward up the Right Hand Road as far as point D.17.c.4.4. with relays at D.17.d.3.0. and D.24.a.3.8. to clear the Right Sector.
A second Ford car was pushed forward to the fork of the road at D.10.d.4.3. and sheltered behind the house. The Middle Sector was cleared to this point through a Bearer Relay post established at D.11.b.0.2.
The Left Sector was cleared through Bearer Relay posts at D.11.a. 4.8. and D.5.b.0.4.
Relays of Bearers were also kept posted along the car routes should the cars be unable to proceed.

APPENDIX C.

Phase 1.
As the advance proceeded further the R.A.Ps were changed to the following:
5th West Rid. Regt and 2/4th Hants Regt. V.30.c.2.8.
ST.PYTHON.
2/4th West Rid. Regt: D.11.b.4.3. later D.6.a.3.5.
2/4th York and Lancs.   D.12.c.7.6. (no change).

On the Right Sector a Ford Car was pushed forward to Point D.24.a.3.8. just short of the railway. (It was not able to cross here as yet the road beyond being too bad). a Bearer Relay of two squads being stationed at D.18.d.0.4. The Middle Sector was cleared as before through Relay Post at D.11.b.0.2. On the Left Sector a Daimler Post was established at D.10.d.4.3. where two squads were stationed for loading purposes. the squads at Relay D.5.d.0.4. being pushed forward into St.PYTHON.to point D.6.a.4.7. in the square, to R.A.P. of 2/4th West Riding Regt. A Relay was placed at D.6.a.1.6. for 5th West Riding Regt. Ford Cars patrolled the roads pushing forward as far as possible, eventually getting to point D.5.d.2.8. near the railway bridge(debris from bridges not yet cleared away) a squad being stationed here as loading party. A forward car control was established at point D.16.c.2.4. near the orchard.

Phase 2.   About this time the 185th Infantry Brigade passed through the 186th Infantry Brigade and a common R.A.P. for the three battns. (8th West Yorks Regt., 2/20th London Regt. and 1/5th Devon Regt) was established at the Factory at point E.7.a.8.0. Horse Ambulances were now taking the Walking Wounded from the A.D.S. straight to M.D.S.

Phase 3.   Later the R.A.Ps were moved into the Church Square SOLESMES about E.1.c.5.3. The debris of bridge at point D.5.b.7.1. was cleared up and a car post established in the central square of ST.PYTHON, Eventually cars were able to proceed as far as the Church Square SOLESMES via D.6.b and d. and collect direct from R.A.Ps.

Confidential

War Diary
of
2/2 West Riding Field Ambce
from 1 Oct 1918 to 31 Oct. 1918

Volume 22

ORIGINAL

"Confidential"   MEDICAL

Vol 23

War Diary

of

2/2nd West Riding Field Ambulance

from 1st Nov. 1918 to 30th November 1918

Volume 23

2/2ND WEST RIDING
FIELD AMBULANCE,
R.A.M.C.

No. ....
Date ....

COMMITTEE FOR THE
MEDICAL HISTORY OF THIS WAR
Date 10 JAN

MEDICAL

Army Form C. 2118.

WAR DIARY
or
INTELLIGENCE SUMMARY.
(Erase heading not required.)

Instructions regarding War Diaries and Intelligence Summaries are contained in F.S. Regs, Part II. and the Staff Manual respectively. Title pages will be prepared in manuscript.

Place	Date	Hour	Summary of Events and Information	Remarks and references to Appendices
QUIEVY	1.XI.18		The Unit is quartered here in billets. Nothing to Report	W.L
QUIEVY	2.XI.18		The Unit proceeded to ESCARMAIN & took over the M.D.S. there from the 7" Field Amb. 3rd Div. 1/LIEUT A.A. STOLL USA M.C returned to this unit from the 2/4 W.Riding Regt. & was replaced by CAPT A. MITCHELL (RAMC(T)) This sprang a number attached to each of the Battalions of the 185 Brigade	W.L W.L
ESCARMAIN	3.XI.18		LIEUT J.H. GRAFF USA MC join'd this unit from pre duty	W.L
ESCARMAIN	4.XI.18		The M.D.S closed down here & opened up at ORSINVAL	W.L
ESCARMAIN	5.XI.18		This unit proceeded to RUESNES & was billeted there	W.L
RUESNES	6.XI.18		Nothing to Report.	W.L
RUESNES	7.XI.18		This unit proceeded to COMMEGNIES & was billeted there for the night	W.L
COMMEGNIES	8.XI.18		This unit proceeded to OBIES & opened a M.D.S there at the Mairie.	W.L
~~COMMEGNIES~~ OBIES	9.XI.18		Nothing to Report.	W.L
~~COMMEGNIES~~ OBIES	10.XI.18		The M.D.S here closed down at noon & another being opened at CHÊNE AU LOUP at the Ferm	W.L
OBIES	11.XI.18		This Unit proceeded to SOUS LE BOIS & entering into billet at the HOSPICE there	W.L

T2134. Wt. W708-776. 500000. 4/15. Sir J. C. & B.

2/2nd WEST RIDING
FIELD AMBULANCE
R.A.M.C.

Army Form C. 2118.

WAR DIARY
or
INTELLIGENCE SUMMARY.
(Erase heading not required.)

Instructions regarding War Diaries and Intelligence Summaries are contained in F. S. Regs., Part II. and the Staff Manual respectively. Title pages will be prepared in manuscript.

Place	Date	Hour	Summary of Events and Information	Remarks and references to Appendices
SOUS LE BOIS	12.XI.18		CAPT S.J.W. DONALD RAMC (TC) reported to this unit for duty. The apparatus attached to the Infantry battalion returns to the unit. A medical Inspection room was opened at these Headquarters for the treatment of CIVILIANS.	ad
SOUS LE BOIS	13.XI.18		Nothing to report	ad
SOUS LE BOIS	14.X.18		1/LIEUTs A.A. STOLL + J.H. GRAFF M.C. USA reported to the ADMS 3rd DIV. for duty and are struck off the strength of this unit. The tent subdivision has been doing duty with the 59 C.C.S. returns to the unit.	ad
SOUS LE BOIS	15.XI.18		Nothing to report	ad
SOUS LE BOIS	16.XI.18		Seeing that the Division is under orders to proceed with the VI CORPS towards the RHINE, the unit was inspected medically & 12 men who were considered unfit to march any great distance were picked out to be left behind with others of the DIV similarly selected. CAPT. A. MITCHELL RAMC (T) rejoined the unit from temporary duty as M.O. i/c 2/4 West Riding Rey/=	ad
SOUS LE BOIS	17.XI.18		Nothing to report	ad

2/2nd WEST RIDING
FIELD AMBULANCE
R.A.M.C.

Army Form C. 2118.

WAR DIARY
or
INTELLIGENCE SUMMARY.
(Erase heading not required.)

Instructions regarding War Diaries and Intelligence Summaries are contained in F. S. Regs., Part II. and the Staff Manual respectively. Title pages will be prepared in manuscript.

Place	Date	Hour	Summary of Events and Information	Remarks and references to Appendices
SOUS LE BOIS	18. XI. 18		This unit proceeded under Bridge arrangements with the 186 Inf Brigade on its proper towards the Rhine & arrived at COLLERET & was billeted there for the night.	
COLLERET	19. XI. 18		We continued the march & arrived at BIERCÉE & billeted for the night.	
BIERCÉE	20. XI. 18		This unit proceeded with 186 Brigade & arrived at SOMZÉE. As we were the first of any British troops to arrive at this village the scene prol rejoicing. The church & bells were rung & the inhabitants turned out to welcome us & several bouquets of flowers were presented to the Colonel & officers. The inhabitants vied with one another in making us welcome, the day school was closed for the day & several schoolboys made visits & a concert in the evening.	
SOMZÉE	21. XI. 18		A letter of appreciation was sent to the Burgomaster of Somzée. Nothing to Report. Unit resting.	
SOMZÉE	22. XI. 18		Under orders of the A.D.M.S. MAJOR DAVIE & CAPT RONALD dispute with motor orderlies, 2 Motor ambulances & some medical equipment proceeded to CINEY it being reported that several sick & wounded had been left behind by the GERMANS upon their evacuation of the area in front of the RIVER MEUSE.	

2/2ND WEST RIDING
FIELD AMBULANCE.

Army Form C. 2118.

No. ....
Date ....

WAR DIARY
or
INTELLIGENCE SUMMARY.
(Erase heading not required.)

Instructions regarding War Diaries and Intelligence Summaries are contained in F. S. Regs., Part II. and the Staff Manual respectively. Title pages will be prepared in manuscript.

Place	Date	Hour	Summary of Events and Information	Remarks and references to Appendices
SOMZÉE	23-XI-18		Nothing to report.	and
NOWECHAMPS	24-XI-18		Unit continued march to the RHINE and arrived NOWECHAMPS — billeted there for the night.	and
BIOUL	25-XI-18		Unit again proceeded E. to Bioul — in billets for the night.	and
EVREHAILLES	26-XI-18		March continued to EVREHAILLES — billeted until next morning.	and
REUX	27-XI-18		Marched to REUX and the ambulance billeted in THE CHATEAU.	and
REUX	28-XI-18		Capt. DONALD with 4 O.R. returned from 62nd Divisional Mobile Medical Unit which, under A.D.M.S. orders had been searching forward area for derelict sick British prisoners of war left behind by the GERMANS.	and
REUX	29-XI-18		Major DAVIE with remainder of above Mobile Unit, 2 ambulances and medical stores reported back. This Mobile Column explored the area from CINEY EAST to VIELSALM. Was relieved by similar detachment from 3rd Division on 28-XI-18. Only 1 sick British prisoner was found and evacuated but 101 French prisoners were treated in improvised hospitals latrine often by Belgian Red Cross under trying conditions. The sick were in terrible state of dirt- and overcrowding. the "BOSCHE" having "dumped" them any where whence they were collected by the BELGIANS and given the best treatment possible under the circumstances.	and

WAR DIARY
or
INTELLIGENCE SUMMARY.

(Erase heading not required.)

2/2ND WEST RIDING
FIELD AMBULANCE.
Army Form C. 2118.

Place	Date	Hour	Summary of Events and Information	Remarks and references to Appendices
REUX	30.xi.16		Nothing to report.	

A.M. Davis
Major R.A.M.C.

LIEUT.-COL. R.A.M.C.
COMDG. 2/2nd WEST RIDING FIELD AMBULANCE.

62 DIV

Box 2934

2/3rd West Riding F.A.

14 0/5481

COMMITTEE FOR THE
MEDICAL HISTORY OF THE WAR
Date 6 MAR 1919

MEDICAL

Army Form C. 2118.

2/2ND WEST RIDING
FIELD AMBULANCE,
R.A.M.C.

WAR DIARY
or
INTELLIGENCE SUMMARY.
(Erase heading not required.)

ORIGINAL

Instructions regarding War Diaries and Intelligence Summaries are contained in F. S. Regs., Part II. and the Staff Manual respectively. Title pages will be prepared in manuscript.

Place	Date	Hour	Summary of Events and Information	Remarks and references to Appendices
REUX	1 - XII - 18		NIL to report.	Annd.
REUX	2 - XII - 18		NIL to report.	Annd.
REUX	3 - XII - 18		NIL to report.	Annd.
REUX	4 - XII - 18		Capt MITCHELL, N.C.O. and 7 men of this unit proceeded to 44 C.C.S. NAMUR for temporary duty.	Annd.
REUX	5 - XII - 18		NIL to report.	Annd.
REUX	6 - XII - 18		NIL to report.	Annd.
REUX	7 - XII - 18		NIL to report.	Annd.
REUX	8 - XII - 18		NIL to report.	Annd.
REUX	9 - XII - 18		NIL to report.	Annd.

Army Form C. 2118.

2/2ND WEST RIDING
FIELD AMBULANCE
R.A.M.C.

WAR DIARY
or
INTELLIGENCE SUMMARY.
(Erase heading not required.)

Instructions regarding War Diaries and Intelligence Summaries are contained in F. S. Regs., Part II. and the Staff Manual respectively. Title pages will be prepared in manuscript.

Place	Date	Hour	Summary of Events and Information	Remarks and references to Appendices
SCY	10-XII-18		Unit left REUX CHATEAU 8:15 a.m. and marched N.E. to SCY — billeted in CHATEAU FARM for one night.	and
CHARDENEUX	11-XII-18		Marched from SCY with 186 Inf Bde group to CHARDENEUX arriving there 11:35 a.m. Remained until next morning.	and
VILLE	12-XII-18		Continued the march to VILLE and arrived 2:30 p.m. In billets one night.	and
HABIMONT	13-XII-18		March resumed and HABIMONT reached 12 p.m. Rested for the night.	and
ENNAL	14-XII-18		Unit proceeded under 186 Inf Bde arrangements S.E. to ENNAL arriving 2:35 p.m. and staying the night.	and
ENNAL	15-XII-18		Rested at ENNAL — NIL to report.	and
POTEAU	16-XII-18		Journey towards RHINE resumed and arrived POTEAU on GERMAN FRONTIER remaining overnight.	and
MIRFELD	17-XII-18		The unit marched into GERMANY and billeted at MIRFELD. Capt. MITCHELL R.A.M.C. and 8 O.R. reported back from 44 C.C.S.	and
MIRFELD	18-XII-18		Nil to report.	and
MIRFELD	19-XII-18		Nil to report.	and
MIRFELD	20-XII-18		Nil to report.	and

WAR DIARY
or
INTELLIGENCE SUMMARY.
(Erase heading not required.)

Army Form C. 2118.

Instructions regarding War Diaries and Intelligence Summaries are contained in F. S. Regs, Part II. and the Staff Manual respectively. Title pages will be prepared in manuscript.

2/2ND WEST RIDING FIELD AMBULANCE. R.A.M.C.

Place	Date	Hour	Summary of Events and Information	Remarks and references to Appendices
NIRFELD	21-XII-18		Nil to report	anid
BULLINGEN	22-XII-18		March resumed to BULLINGEN and unit remained there one night.	anid
HELLENTHAL	23-XII-18		Proceeding N.E. HELLENTHAL was reached 2pm. Remained the night there.	anid
HEISTERT	24-XII-18		With 186 Inf. Bde group march resumed to HEISTERT. In billets until following morning.	anid
HOLZHEIM	25-XII-18		March continued to HOLZHEIM and the AMBULANCE billeted there.	anid
HOLZHEIM	26-XII-18		Detention Hospital opened by this unit in village school with accommodation for 20 beds for sick from 186 Inf Bde group and R.F.A. group. 1 Cpl. and 15 men reposened the unit from 62nd Div Wing.	anid
HOLZHEIM	27-XII-18		Nil to report.	anid
HOLZHEIM	28-XII-18		Capt. DONALD R.A.M.C. left unit on LEAVE to IRELAND.	anid
HOLZHEIM	29-XII-18		6 O.R. (COALMINERS) sent to U.K. for DEMOBILISATION.	anid
			1 O.R. (longest service in a THEATRE OF WAR) sent to U.K. for DEMOBILISATION.	
			1 O.R. (POLICE) sent to U.K. to "DEMOBILISER".	
HOLZHEIM	30-XII-18		2 O.R. (COALMINERS) sent to U.K. for DEMOBILISATION.	anid
HOLZHEIM	31-XII-18		NIL TO REPORT.	anid

C. Anderson
Lieut. Colonel, R.A.M.C.(T)
Commanding 2/2nd W.R. Field Ambulance

140/3490

2/Lieut Aker Roung F.a.

Jan 1919

"MEDICAL"

Army Form C. 2118.

WAR DIARY
or
INTELLIGENCE SUMMARY.
(Erase heading not required.)

Instructions regarding War Diaries and Intelligence Summaries are contained in F.S. Regs., Part II. and the Staff Manual respectively. Title pages will be prepared in manuscript.

ORIGINAL

Place	Date	Hour	Summary of Events and Information	Remarks and references to Appendices
HOLZHEIM	1.1.19		The unit is billeted here in the houses. A detention Hospital was opened at fuel in the village school but late mans to the dancing Hall. The Main Xmas dinner with refreshments & Concert was held today as the Unit was on the march on Xmas day. Lt Col C.W. EAMES RAMC(T) proceeded on leave to the UK from Jany 1st to Jany 15th. Also awarded the D.S.O.	aa aa aa aa
HOLZHEIM	2.1.19		Nothing to Report	
HOLZHEIM	3.1.19		Nothing to Report	
HOLZHEIM	4.1.19		Nothing to Report	
HOLZHEIM	5.1.19		3. OR (long service men) sent to UK for demobilization. Capt G.G. JACK RAMC (SR) awarded the Military Cross, also proceeded to take up the post of DADMS 62nd Division with the acting rank of MAJOR	aa aa
HOLZHEIM	6.1.19		Nothing to Report	
HOLZHEIM	7.1.19		MAJOR A.M DAVIE RAMC(T) together with 6 OR. & 3 MAC cars proceeded to COLOGNE where similar parties were collecting with a view to proceeding into GERMANY searching the towns & villages for abandoned wounded Prisoners of War, sick or wounded who had not been repatriated	aa

Army Form C. 2118.

WAR DIARY
of
INTELLIGENCE SUMMARY.

(Erase heading not required.)

Instructions regarding War Diaries and Intelligence
Summaries are contained in F. S. Regs., Part II.
and the Staff Manual respectively. Title pages
will be prepared in manuscript.

Place	Date	Hour	Summary of Events and Information	Remarks and references to Appendices
HOLZHEIM	8.1.19		Educational classes commenced in the unit Authentic Shooting, Bookbinding being the principle ones to begin with. The scheme laid out is to keep the classes as much as possible in the mornings, the men attending becoming all fatigues etc for the purpose, the afternoon as far as possible are devoted to Recreational training (inter unit football matches, cross country inter coy drives, details etc	
			the endeavour to concerts, whist drives etc	aa
HOLZHEIM	9.1.19		Nothing to Report	aa
HOLZHEIM	10.1.19		Nothing to Report	aa
HOLZHEIM	11.1.19		Nothing to Report	aa
HOLZHEIM	12.1.19		Nothing to Report	aa
HOLZHEIM	13.1.19		5 OR proceeded to U.K. for demobilisation.	aa
HOLZHEIM	14.1.19		Nothing to Report	aa
HOLZHEIM	15.1.19		Nothing to Report	aa
HOLZHEIM	16.1.19		Nothing to Report	aa
HOLZHEIM	17.1.19		Nothing to Report	aa
HOLZHEIM	18.1.19		Nothing to Report.	aa

WAR DIARY or INTELLIGENCE SUMMARY.

Army Form C. 2118.

Instructions regarding War Diaries and Intelligence Summaries are contained in F. S. Regs., Part II. and the Staff Manual respectively. Title pages will be prepared in manuscript.

(Erase heading not required.)

Place	Date	Hour	Summary of Events and Information	Remarks and references to Appendices
HOLZHEIM	19.1.19		Nothing to Report	aa
HOLZHEIM	20.1.19		Nothing to Report	aa
HOLZHEIM	21.1.19		Nothing to Report	aa
HOLZHEIM	22.1.19		CAPT S.J.W. DONALD RAMC (TC) proceeded to the 2/4 YORK & LANC Regt for temporary duty as M.O.	aa
HOLZHEIM	23.1.19		Nothing to Report	aa
HOLZHEIM	24.1.19		Nothing to Report	aa
HOLZHEIM	25.1.19		CAPT A. MITCHELL RAMC (T) proceeded to the U.K. for 14 days leave. CAPT C.O. BODMAN RAMC (TC) reported to the unit for temporary duty from No. 47 C.C.S	aa
HOLZHEIM	26.1.19		Nothing to Report	aa
HOLZHEIM	27.1.19		Nothing to Report	aa
HOLZHEIM	28.1.19		Nothing to Report	aa
HOLZHEIM	29.1.19		Nothing to Report	aa
HOLZHEIM	30.1.19		Nothing to Report	aa
HOLZHEIM	31.1.19		Nothing to Report	aa

A. Anderson
Major RAMC(T)

C W Dunne
LIEUT.-COL., R.A.M.C.
COMDG. 2/2nd WEST RIDING FIELD AMBULANCE.

Feb. 1919.

'40/3624'

Confidential

War Diary

of

2/2nd West Riding Field Ambulance

From 1st February to 28th February 1919.

Volume 21

MEDICAL

Army Form C. 2118.

WAR DIARY
or
INTELLIGENCE SUMMARY.
(Erase heading not required.)

2/2nd West Riding Field Ambulance.

WD 26

Instructions regarding War Diaries and Intelligence Summaries are contained in F. S. Regs., Part II. and the Staff Manual respectively. Title pages will be prepared in manuscript.

Place	Date	Hour	Summary of Events and Information	Remarks and references to Appendices
HOLZHEIM	1/2/19		The unit is still engaged in the town of this village. A DETENTION HOSPITAL is working in a room previously used as a brewing house, with a special ANNEXE for segregated cases. A BLUE LAMP ROOM is also established in the village with all necessary equipment for prophylactic treatment. CAPT. C. BODMAN RAMC (TC) attached to this unit for temporary duty was ordered for duty to 44 CCS at COLOGNE.	
HOLZHEIM	2.II.19		Nothing to Report.	
HOLZHEIM	3.II.19		Nothing to Report.	
HOLZHEIM	4.II.19		Under the EDUCATIONAL SCHEME 5 OR. visited the TECHNICAL TEXTILE SCHOOL at AACHEN & also were shewn round the principal Textile works of that town.	
HOLZHEIM	5.II.19		One OR. (RASC) PIVOTAL (Iron Smelter) proceeded to the U.K for DEMOBILIZATION	
HOLZHEIM	6.II.19		Nothing to Report	
HOLZHEIM	7.II.19		MAJOR A.M. DAVIE, RAMC (TF) Seven OR 93 MAC amb car returned from the INTERIOR of GERMANY where they had been today spent in a systematic search of the country for any ALLIED P(risoners) of WAR who might still be remaining about, sick or otherwise detained.	

Army Form C. 2118.

WAR DIARY
or
INTELLIGENCE SUMMARY.
(Erase heading not required.)

2/2nd West Riding Field Ambulance.

Place	Date	Hour	Summary of Events and Information	Remarks and references to Appendices
HOLZHEIM	8.II.19		Nothing to Report	do
HOLZHEIM	9.II.19		Nothing to Report	do
HOLZHEIM	10.II.19		Nothing to Report	do
HOLZHEIM	11.II.19		Nothing to Report	do
HOLZHEIM	12.II.19		Nothing to Report	do
HOLZHEIM	13.II.19		Nothing to Report	do
HOLZHEIM	14.II.19		Owing to the revision of the Establishment of a Field Amb, the following vehicles were handed over to Ordnance. 1 AMB WAGON. 1 GS WAGON. one WATER CART. (one LIMBER G.S. being retained awaiting instruction as to disposal)	do
HOLZHEIM	15.II.19		One OR (AGRICULTURIST) proceeded to the U.K. for DEMOBILIZATION	do
HOLZHEIM	16.II.19		Nothing to Report	do
HOLZHEIM	17.II.19		Nothing to Report	do
HOLZHEIM	18.II.19		Nothing to Report	do
HOLZHEIM	19.II.19		One OR (RASC) (AGRICULTURIST) proceeded to the U.K. for DEMOBILIZATION	do
HOLZHEIM	20.II.19		Nothing to Report	do

Army Form C. 2118.

WAR DIARY
or
INTELLIGENCE SUMMARY.
(Erase heading not required.)

2/2nd West Riding Field Ambulance.

Instructions regarding War Diaries and Intelligence Summaries are contained in F. S. Regs., Part II. and the Staff Manual respectively. Title pages will be prepared in manuscript.

Place	Date	Hour	Summary of Events and Information	Remarks and references to Appendices
HOLZHEIM	21 II 19		Owing to the revision of the ESTABLISHMENT of FIELD AMBULANCES the numbers of ANIMALS have been taken from the unit viz - 2 Riders, four H.D Rovers & 4 mules leaving 5 Riders, 16 H.D Rovers & 13 mules. Also A/MAJOR A.M DAVIE RAMC(TF) relinquishes his acting rank of Major upon the establishment of ACTING MAJORS being reduced from two to one.	
			Three O.R. (RASC) (LONG SERVICE) proceeded to U.K for DEMOBILIZATION	OR
HOLZHEIM	22 II 19		Nothing to Report.	OR
HOLZHEIM	23 II 19		CAPT. S.J.W. DONALD RAMC (TC) returned to this unit from temporary duty as M.O with the 2/4 YORK & LANCS Regt	OR
HOLZHEIM	24 II 19		Nothing to Report	OR
HOLZHEIM	25 II 19		Nothing to Report	OR
HOLZHEIM	26 II 19		Nothing to Report	OR
HOLZHEIM	27 II 19		One O.R. (RAMC)(PIVOTAL) proceeded to the U.K for DEMOBILIZATION.	OR
HOLZHEIM	28 II 19		Nothing to Report	OR

A. Anderson (TF)
Major RAMC (TF)

C. W Raws
LIEUT.-COL., R.A.M.C.,
COMDG. 2/2nd WEST RIDING FIELD AMBULANCE.

160/3551

27 JUL 1919

2/Lt. W. Dickey 7.U.

Nov. 1919

Medical

WAR DIARY
or
INTELLIGENCE SUMMARY.
(Erase heading not required.)

Army Form C. 2118.

2/2nd West Riding Field Ambulance.

WO/27

Place	Date	Hour	Summary of Events and Information	Remarks and references to Appendices
HOLZHEIM	1.III.19		The unit is in billets in this village. A DETENTION HOSPITAL is running in a school previously used as a lunatic hall, whilst a special arrangement is being made. A BLUE LAMP room is also established in the village. There are necessary equipment for prophylactic treatment.	aga
HOLZHEIM	2.III.19		Nothing to report	aa
HOLZHEIM	3.III.19		Nothing to report	aa
HOLZHEIM	4.III.19		CAPT A. MITCHELL RAMC (TF) appointed EDUCATION OFFICER to the unit. CPL R.F. THOMAS & PTE T.L. SWALLOW were sent to work at the school.	aa
HOLZHEIM	5.III.19		LT COL C.W. EAMES RAMC(TF) proceeded to DIV HQ as acting ADMS upon P. ADMS being demobilised. CAPT S.J.W. DONALD proceeds to 2/2 W.R. Field Amb for temporary duty	aa
HOLZHEIM	6.III.19		Nothing to report	aa
HOLZHEIM	7.III.19		Nothing to report	aa
HOLZHEIM	8.III.19		One O.R. (NT) proceeded to U.K. for demobilization	aa
HOLZHEIM	9.III.19		Nothing to report	aa

WAR DIARY or INTELLIGENCE SUMMARY

Army Form C. 2118.
2/2nd West Riding Field Ambulance

Place	Date	Hour	Summary of Events and Information	Remarks and references to Appendices
HOLZHEIM	10.III.19	19	Nothing to Report	aa
HOLZHEIM	11.III.19	19	The unit together with its transport proceeded by road to MECHERNICH where they entrained & proceeded by rail to VETTWEISS where detrained & marching by road to KELZ where the unit went into billets.	aa
KELZ	12.III.19	19	A DETENTION HOSPITAL establishe also a BLUE LAMP ROOM. Bespoke accommodation.	aa
KELZ	13.III.19	19	LT COL CW.EAMES R.A.M.C.(T.F) D.S.O & CAPT.A.M.DAVIE R.A.M.C.(T.F) proceeded to UK for demobilisation.	aa
KELZ	14.III.19	19	Lieut J.N. (PIS ALLAN) A.S.C. proceeded to UK for demobilisation	aa
KELZ	15.III.19	19	Nothing to Report	aa
KELZ	16.III.19	19	Nothing to Report	aa
KELZ	17.III.19	19	Nothing to Report	aa
KELZ	18.III.19	19	CAPT H.G. DODD R.A.M.C.(T.F) reported for duty and was taken on strength	aa
KELZ	19.III.19	19	CAPT A/MAJOR A. ANDERSON R.A.M.C.(T.F) proceeded to hospital station for demobilisation	aa
KELZ	20.III.19	19	CAPT H.G. DODD R.A.M.C.(T.F) proceed to report to War Office, LONDON. CAPT. J.H.W. DYKE R.A.M.C.(T.C.) reported for duty and was taken on strength	aa
KELZ	21.III.19	19	CAPT. (B.SC.) KEMP R.A.M.C. (S.R.) reported for duty and was taken on strength	aa

Army Form C. 2118.

WAR DIARY
or
INTELLIGENCE SUMMARY.
(Erase heading not required.)

2/2nd West Riding Field Ambulance.

Instructions regarding War Diaries and Intelligence Summaries are contained in F.S. Regs., Part II. and the Staff Manual respectively. Title pages will be prepared in manuscript.

Place	Date	Hour	Summary of Events and Information	Remarks and references to Appendices
KELZ	22.III.19		CAPT. H.N. DYKE R.A.M.C.(T.C.) proceeded to report to 5th GORDON H. units LIZEU after change of the unit	Apy
KELZ	23.III.19		Nothing to report	Apy
KELZ	24.III.19		Nothing to report	Apy
KELZ	25.III.19		Nothing to report	Apy
KELZ	26.III.19		Nothing to report	Apy
KELZ	27.III.19		CAPT. T. KENWORTHY R.A.M.C. (T.F.) reported to out look Command this unit.	Apy
KELZ	28.3.19		Nothing to report	30k
KELZ	29.3.19		CAPT. S.T. M. DONALD R.A.M.C (F.C.) is taken off this unit. Struck being transferred to 1/3 W.R.F.A.	30k
KELZ	30.3.19		Nothing to report	20k
KELZ	31.3.19		Divisional Scabies Hospital was opened	22k

D.Kenworthy Captain R.A.M.C.
COMDG. 2/2nd WEST RIDING FIELD AMBULANCE.

CONFIDENTIAL

WAR DIARY

OF

2/2nd. WEST RIDING FIELD AMBULANCE.

From 1st. April, 1919 to 30th April 1919.

VOLUME No. 28.

Germany/Nov I L. 1/10000

MEDICAL
Army Form C. 2118.

2/2ND WEST RIDING
FIELD AMBULANCE,
R.A.M.C.

No. ....
Date ....

WAR DIARY
or
INTELLIGENCE SUMMARY.
(Erase heading not required.)

Instructions regarding War Diaries and Intelligence
Summaries are contained in F. S. Regs., Part II.
and the Staff Manual respectively. Title pages
will be prepared in manuscript.

Place	Date	Hour	Summary of Events and Information	Remarks and references to Appendices
KELZ	1.4.19		The unit is still at KELZ in Germany in charge of a Group Reception Hospital & Divisional Scabies. CAPT. G.S.L. KEMP R.A.M.C. proceeded to GEY for temporary duty with 136 SB. R.G.A	
KELZ	3.4.19		CAPT. G.S.L. KEMP R.A.M.C. returned from temp'y duty with 136 SB R.G.A	9K
KELZ	5.4.19		and returned to the Battery for further temp'y duty	9K
KELZ	6.4.19		Nothing to report	9K
KELZ	7.4.19		Nothing to report	9K
KELZ	8.4.19		CAPT W K CHURCHOUSE R.A.M.C. T/F is taken on the strength of this unit as from 17.3.19 is posted to No 2 Concentration (Army) Camp for duty	9K
KELZ	9.4.19		CAPT G.S.L KEMP returned this unit from temp'y duty with 168 SB R.G.A. The unit moves to DUREN & took over a portion of the LEHOER SEMINAR. This opens a Brigade & Corps Troops Detention Hospital also a detention hospital for Scabies of Highland Division	9K
DUREN	10.4.19		Nothing to report	9K
DUREN	11.4.19		Nothing to report	9K
DUREN	12.4.19		CAPT A MITCHELL R.A.M.C. (T/F) proceeded to U.K. for demobilisation	9K

(A9175) Wt W2353/P363 60,000 12/17 D.D. & L. Sch. 53a. Forms/C2118/15.

Army Form C. 2118.

2/2ND WEST RIDING
FIELD AMBULANCE,
R.A.M.C.

WAR DIARY
or
INTELLIGENCE SUMMARY.
(Erase heading not required.)

Instructions regarding War Diaries and Intelligence Summaries are contained in F. S. Regs., Part II. and the Staff Manual respectively. Title pages will be prepared in manuscript.

Place	Date	Hour	Summary of Events and Information	Remarks and references to Appendices
DUREN	12/4/19		CAPT. J.W. MALCOLM M.C. RAMC (S.R.) reported for duty	JMc
DUREN	13/4/19		Nothing to report	JMc
DUREN	14/4/19		A small number of civilian infectious hospital in the vicinity was taken over for the accommodation of Small Pox contacts expected to arrive	JMc
			In quarantine from the ST VITH - MALMEDY area	JMc
DUREN	15/4/19		CAPT. J.W. HARCOURT MC RAMC proceeded to 1/4 Gordon Highlanders for	JMc
			temporary duty as M.O.	JMc
DUREN	16/4/19		LIEUT. +Q.M. F.W. NEWBOULT returned from leave to U.K.	JMc
DUREN	17/4/19		Nothing to report	JMc
DUREN	18/4/19		Nothing to report	JMc
DUREN	19/4/19		Nothing to report	JMc
DUREN	20/4/19		Nothing to report	JMc
DUREN	21/4/19		D.M.S Army of the Rhine accompanied by Inspector General of Medical Services visited the M.S. Ambulance to inspect the treatment of Scabies	JMc
DUREN	22/4/19		O.C. Unit visited Cologne to attend a conference called by D.M.S. Inspector General. The health of the young soldiers was generally discussed	JMc

Army Form C. 2118.

2/2nd WEST RIDING
FIELD AMBULANCE,
R.A.M.C.

No. ....
Date ....

WAR DIARY
or
INTELLIGENCE SUMMARY.
(Erase heading not required.)

Instructions regarding War Diaries and Intelligence Summaries are contained in F. S. Regs., Part II. and the Staff Manual respectively. Title pages will be prepared in manuscript.

Place	Date	Hour	Summary of Events and Information	Remarks and references to Appendices
DUREN	23/4/19		Nothing to report	2/2
DUREN	24/4/19		Nothing to report	2/2
DUREN	25/4/19		CAPT G.S. KEMP RAMC attached 2nd Royal Scots Fusiliers on Education	2/2
DUREN	26/4/19		Nothing to report	2/2
DUREN	27/4/19		Nothing to report	2/2
DUREN	28/4/19		Nothing to report	2/2
DUREN	29/4/19		12 OR reinforcements arrived for duty	2/2
DUREN	30/4/19		Small-Pox contacts expected on the 14th have not yet arrived	2/2

J. Hemsworth
Captain
LIEUT-COL., R.A.M.C.,
COMDG. 2/2nd WEST RIDING FIELD AMBULANCE.

Medical

May '19

CONFIDENTIAL.

WAR DIARY

of

2/2nd. WEST RIDING FIELD AMBULANCE RAMC(TF).

from
1st MAY 1919
to
31st MAY 1919

VOLUME No 29.

Army Form C. 2118.

2/2nd WEST RIDING
FIELD AMBULANCE,
R.A.M.C.

Medical

WAR DIARY

INTELLIGENCE SUMMARY.

(Erase heading not required.)

Instructions regarding War Diaries and Intelligence Summaries are contained in F. S. Regs., Part II, and the Staff Manual respectively. Title pages will be prepared in manuscript.

Place	Date	Hour	Summary of Events and Information	Remarks and references to Appendices
DUREN	1.5.19		The unit is still continuing to run Divisional Scabies Hospital & Brigade Delousing Hosp. at Felsbahn Schreiner Duren Germany	
DUREN	2.5.19			WK
DUREN	3.5.19			
DUREN	4.5.19			
DUREN	5.5.19		Nothing to report	WK
DUREN	6.5.19			
DUREN	7.5.19			
DUREN	8.5.19		1 NCO & 4 OR RAMC + 1 Dr HT Rasc paraded at 36 CCS Köln for inspection by Field Marshall HRH The Duke of Connaught KG Col. in Chief RAMC G.O.C IV Corps DDMS inspected his hospitals	WK
DUREN	9.5.19			WK
DUREN	10.5.19			
DUREN	11.5.19			WK
DUREN	12.5.19		Nothing to report	
DUREN	13.5.19			

Army Form C. 2118.

WAR DIARY
or
INTELLIGENCE SUMMARY.
(Erase heading not required.)

Instructions regarding War Diaries and Intelligence Summaries are contained in F. S. Regs., Part II. and the Staff Manual respectively. Title pages will be prepared in manuscript.

[Stamp: 2 2ND WEST RIDING FIELD AMBULANCE, R.A.M.C.]

Place	Date	Hour	Summary of Events and Information	Remarks and references to Appendices
DUREN	14.6.19		Nothing to report	QM
DUREN	15.6.19		The C in C British Army of the Rhine inspected the 2nd Highland Brigade on parade including this unit - at Duren	
DUREN	16.6.19		Nothing to report	QM
DUREN	17.6.19			
DUREN	18.6.19			QM
DUREN	19.6.19		2) Privates of the 37th Gordon Highlanders reported for duty for instruction in transport duties	
DUREN	20.6.19		Nothing to report	QM
DUREN	21.6.19			
DUREN	22.6.19			
DUREN	23.6.19		This unit handed over all duties at Lechler Caserne to 43 F.A. 20 Ambces. moved by road to GIRBELSRATH. Notification received that under instructions from G.H.Q. the ambulance is to be disbanded	30K
GIRBELSRATH DULREN	24.5.19		Nothing to report	

Army Form C. 2118.

WAR DIARY
or
INTELLIGENCE SUMMARY
(Erase heading not required.)

2/2nd WEST RIDING
FIELD AMBULANCE,
R.A.M.C.

No...........
Date.........

Instructions regarding War Diaries and Intelligence Summaries are contained in F. S. Regs., Part II. and the Staff Manual respectively. Title pages will be prepared in manuscript.

Place	Date	Hour	Summary of Events and Information	Remarks and references to Appendices
CIRBEELSRATH	25/5/19		Nothing to report. MM.	
do	26/5/19		Extract from London Gazette of 24/5/19:- Lt.Qm. F.W. NEWBOULT to be Captain, seniority from 8.8. T.F. Reg. (May 15) MM.	
do	27/5/19		Capt. T.R. KENWORTHY proceeded to U.K. for 14 days leave. MM. Nothing to report. MM.	
do	28/5/19			
do	29/5/19		Capt. J.W. MALCOLM R.A.M.C.(S.R.) & Capt. W.K. CHURCHOUSE R.A.M.C.(T.F.) taken off strength of unit. MM.	
do	30/5/19		Nothing to report. MM.	
do	31/5/19			

H. Newboult
Lt. & Qm. R.A.M.C.(T.)
for O.C. 2/2 W.R.F. Amb.

www.ingramcontent.com/pod-product-compliance
Lightning Source LLC
Chambersburg PA
CBHW081357160426
43192CB00013B/2430